ALADE OLUWATOYOSI

START IT UP!

Entrepreneurship Toolkit For Teens And Beginners

Start It Up: Entrepreneurship Toolkit for Teens and Beginners

Copyright © 2024 by Alade Oluwatoyosi

ISBN: 978-978-60907-9-5

Published and printed by:

Pen-Impact Writing and Publishing Enterprise
16 Adedoyin Rhodes-Vivour Close, Asokoro,
Abuja, FCT, Nigeria
Website: www.pen-impact.com
Email: info@pen-impact.com
Tel: +234 701 990 4999

CONTENTS

INTRODUCTION

The rate of unemployment in the countries of the world is quite alarming. According to the Nigeria Bureau of Statistics (NBS), unemployment increased to 7.2% in the second quarter (Q2) of 2023. This shows that many graduates and well-abled youths are unemployed, underemployed or underpaid. Many graduates are busy roaming the streets in search of white-collar jobs that don't really exist; when they fail to find one, they are made to fall back on 'blue-collar jobs' that pay meagre remuneration just because they don't want to stay idle, and they must keep body and soul together.

I see frustration and disappointment on the faces of many of our youths; many are still dependent on parents and the government for financial upkeep and welfare. It is quite pathetic when you see first-degree and master's degree holders earning peanuts that secondary school certificate holders received years back. Many of our graduates are stranded and confused because they were not trained to be self-employed or entrepreneurs. One of the sure ways to go in this economically challenging period is the way of entrepreneurship.

To this end, the Nigerian Government at all levels have seen the need to introduce entrepreneurship programmes in the educational system of students; hence, 'Entrepreneurship' was introduced as a compulsory course in tertiary institutions for all students as a prerequisite to graduation. This was a great step, but entrepreneurship studies should not just start with undergraduates in higher institutions; it should be infused into the country's universal BASIC curriculum in secondary schools in order to catch them young.

Entrepreneurship is not just about training students on how to do the business of buying and selling but how to develop mental capacity so as not to be intimidated by the challenges around them. It should adequately equip students on how to see opportunities, create, invent, innovate and develop new ideas and technologies to solve challenges and make life better for all. Entrepreneurship studies should be designed in a way to help students know how to commercialize their creativity, ingenuity, invention and innovation.

The foundation of entrepreneurship is 'self-discovery'. Self-discovery is the understanding of your personality, your innate qualities such as your talents, abilities, natural gifts and potentials, and acquired knowledge/skills that can determine what you are capable of doing. Entrepreneurship studies help you to understand those things that are embedded in you. This includes developing and deploying them in a way that human needs will be met, problems will be solved, life will become better, and profits will be made.

A lot of talents and opportunities lay waste because most youths have been tailored to be dependent on their academic qualifications and certificates. The objective of this book is to catch young minds early by inculcating in them some principles that can help them on the journey to becoming entrepreneurs, business tycoons, business magnates and business executives. Remember, it is better to train a child than to repair an adult.

This book has been written in a practical and fascinating way to stir the interest of the readers. The principles and knowledge shared are based on the practical experiences of the author and other entrepreneurs. These experiences are presented in a drama form to make them relatable and pleasurable for all. Each chapter covers a unique topic with a different set of characters for the fun of it. It covers secondary school settings, tertiary institutions and marketplaces. I am pretty sure this book will contribute and will revolutionize the way you perceive business.

APPRECIATION

I sincerely want to return all the thanks and praise to the giver of all wisdom and knowledge that made it possible for me to document some of my ideas and thoughts in this book. This book wouldn't have become a reality without the support and sacrifices of my beautiful wife and our lovely angels, Oluwaseun Ibukun Alade, Miracle and Marvelous, thanks my glitters.

I sincerely want to thank my wonderful parents for their love and support always, Pst. (Engr.) J. B. Alade & Mrs. A. A. Alade and my lovely parents in love, Pst. & Pst. (Mrs.) Adepetun. I appreciate Dr. (Mrs.) Abimbola Oshakuade, Pastor Olayinka Akintayo-Job, Angela Evans, Esther Nsaka, Mosope Adebunmi, Tunde Olugbodi, Femi Alade, Yinka Alade and Busola Lijadu.

My appreciation also goes to Lt. Col. B Yusuf, Maj. S. Ali, Mrs. I. Tate and the entire staff of the NAOWA College, Kurudu. I also deeply appreciate Mrs. Salamatu F. Yahaya and Mrs Mariya Abiodun Lagbaja, the former and current president of NAOWA for the platform given to rise.

CHAPTER 1

Business Sense

John: I would like to become an engineer when I grow up, just like Engineer Seyi Makinde, the man who became the governor of Oyo State in 2019.

Ayo: Wow! I have heard about him; he is wealthy and generous. I even heard he is a billionaire.

James: Sure, I heard that too. He started as an engineer in an oil company but now has many companies and businesses of his own.

Bola: But why is he that stupendously rich? What is the secret of his wealth?

John: He has business sense, and he's a serial entrepreneur, I guess.

Bola: What is business sense? Are you saying he knows how to buy and sell?

John: Business sense is not only about buying and selling goods but also being able to trade what you have, such as knowledge, information, ideas, skills, resources or services, in return for money.

Tayo: Can I be a doctor and still become an entrepreneur?

Ayo: That is the same question on my mind; I want to become a scientist. Can I still become a businessman?

Idowu: Is it possible to be a pilot and an entrepreneur too?

Tolu: Does business sense apply to me, as I want to be the first Nigerian to create a combat robot that will go and fight in BattleBots?

John: You see, every profession has a business side to it, whether you are a doctor, an engineer, an accountant, a pilot, a teacher, a nurse or a pharmacist. There are opportunities to do business in all. Jeff Bezos, one of the richest entrepreneurs in the world and the owner of Amazon, is an electrical engineer and computer scientist by profession. Afe Babalola (CON, OFR, SAN) started his career as a lawyer, but today, he is one of the most successful entrepreneurs in Nigeria with study centres, universities, farms and many other ventures. Cristiano Ronaldo, a world-class footballer, has made millions with brand endorsements, his two clothing stores, and a shoe brand called CR7 footwear, and he recently announced that he will soon launch a chain of boutique hotels.

Bayo: So, what is business sense, and how can I become an entrepreneur in my profession?

John: Have you heard of Dr. Ola Orekunrin? She is a medical doctor, helicopter pilot and healthcare entrepreneur. She is the founder of Flying Doctors Nigeria, west Africa's first air ambulance service. She saw the challenge patients encounter in public airlines when they have to be flown abroad for better treatment, and this inspired her business. So basically, one should be able to identify the problems and needs of people and think of how to proffer solutions to them with one's expertise, skills or resources. For example, if you are a teacher and you see that students find it hard to understand your subject, you can develop a game to help students love and easily understand the subject. By so doing, you have solved that problem and can package it to sell to parents. Don't be surprised that the problem can be peculiar to students in general. In summary, Business sense is the ability to use your knowledge, experiences or the resources you have to solve people's problems. The resultant solution is packaged in an appealing way, which brings profits and returns to you.

Bayo: But I don't want to be buying and selling goods because I dislike marketing or selling.

John: You see, you don't need to be involved in buying and selling of goods. Take Ben Carson, for instance; he goes to schools and conferences to educate and enlighten people, packages his life stories and knowledge in books, and makes money. There are many channels through which you can sell your products. His biography has been used to make movies, and I am sure he gets royalties in return.

Idowu: So, the business sense is all about me packaging the knowledge, talents, and skills that I have in a way that will add value and solve problems?

John: Exactly! When your ideas, knowledge are well packaged to solve people's problems, they will be willing to pay for it, that's business sense!

Bayo, Idowu and Bola: Indeed, one must have business sense.

CHAPTER 2

Not Too Young to Start

Bola: Dr. Tayo, Dr. Tayo.

Tayo: Yes, that's me. I am determined to become a successful neurosurgeon like Dr. Ben Carson in the future.

John: Bola, you are the only one among us who is passionate about strictly becoming a successful business tycoon, owning companies, and employing thousands like Aliko Dangote.

Bola: You are right, that is my dream any day, any time. I want to be like Dangote, Femi Otedola, Jeff Bezos, Bill Gates, Elon Musk and the like.

John: How far have you gone with that?

Bola: Hmmm, seriously, I think about that too; I concluded I would launch out and have time for my business when I get admission into the university.

Tayo: I like your dreams and aspirations, but do you know it is never too early to start? My dad always tells us that the future we think about is now. Many people think of a glorious future, but only a few realize that the great future they dream about comes their way day by day, bit by bit.

John: Well, just like TY said, it is never too early to start something in line with one's dream and aspiration, no matter how small. From the story of Dangote that my uncle told me, he started quite early; he was groomed by his uncle, Dantata. At age 8, he started his business by the side. This passion later led him to study business administration, and he was able to get a loan from his uncle to expand his business.

Tayo: His story is similar to that of Warren Buffett; Buffett happened to be the richest man in the world at some point, a mentor to Bill Gates, he, too, started his business at the age of 6, buying sweets and selling to his friends.

Bola: Wow! You guys are really challenging and motivating me.

Tayo: Though there are people who started late in life, too, they made it big before they died. A typical example is Colonel Sanders, who owns KFC. He started at 65, but it is always good to start early so that one will grow on the job with lots of experience to show for it.

John: If one has the means and the passion, it is never too early to start.

Bola: Come to think of it. I already have many ideas of what to do and how to do them, but my mind has been programmed to start when I get to the university.

John: Friend, the earlier you start, the better for you. Don't be shocked that the idea you have may be implemented by another right before your very eyes before you even finish secondary school. The right time to start is now!

Bola: Thank you, guys; I will surely do something about that.

CHAPTER 3

Your Talent – A Source

Ade: Did you listen to the entertainment news on the radio this afternoon?

Kola: Yes, my brain nearly left its skull when I heard the net worth of Davido, Wizkid and others.

Ade: Can you imagine those guys having billions of Naira in their accounts?

Kola: Well, they are talented artists, so I'm not surprised.

Ade: What do you mean by talented artists?

Kola: Talented artists use their natural abilities and innate qualities to entertain, enlighten and educate others through their songs, arts and crafts.

Ade: How I wish I had singing talent just like them.

Kola: Hmm...Ah! Me, I envy people like Cristiano Ronaldo, Lionel Messi, Ramsey Noah, Genevieve Nnaji, and Chimamanda Adiche. These people are young millionaires!

Titi: What are you guys talking about that you look so serious?

Ade: I am not just happy.

Kola: Didn't you hear about the net worth of Nigerian musicians and entertainers generally? Those guys are stupendously wealthy and famous. How I wish I could sing or play football or act in movies or write books like them.

Titi: (smiles) You see, you don't have to compare yourself to any one of them. We have all been endowed with one talent or the other by providence. Some of us can sing, some can act, some can draw and paint, some can cook, some can dance, some can talk, and some can make people laugh. We are all gifted and talented; there is no one without talent and natural potential.

The problem with many of us is that we compare ourselves with others. We wish to have what others have and this beclouds us from making the best of what we have.

Ade: But I think some talents have more prospects than others.

Titi: There is no talent that is not special or unique. Do you know Kaffy, the dancer and choreographer? Can you believe her name has entered the Guinness Book of Records because of her dancing skills? She is a video vixen; she has featured and choreographed in many musical videos, making money out of dance. She has also been a panellist and judge for the MTN Project Fame, Maltina Dance Hall, etc. I am sure you know Mickey Mouse. It was invented by Walt Disney. Walt became very wealthy and renowned because of his drawing and painting skills to the point that he owned Disney Park – an amusement park. Can you imagine the fortune and fame Hilda Bassey enjoys now just because of her 'cookathon'?

Kola: Hmmm, Titi, I am beginning to see sense in what you are saying. People like Wole Soyinka, James Hardley Chase have made fortunes through writing, Fela Durotoye and Les Brown have made fortunes through public speaking and talking, Ali Baba and Kelvin Hart through making people laugh.

Titi: Exactly my point! The most important thing is to discover your talent, which is your innate gift, and your passion – that which you like doing with ease. Celebrate it, develop it and look for ways you can use it to solve people's problems, package it and sell it to people. By the time they buy it, you become happy and make your cool cash.

Ade: I see, so we can trade our talents for money. Let's go there, let me go and discover my talent.

Titi: The mistake many people make is that they wait for opportunity to come first, not knowing that when preparedness meets with opportunities, success is inevitable. So, start preparing now. There is this story of a young boy who drew and painted 2baba (2face); somebody saw it and felt impressed, so he posted it on social media for it to go viral. I was told 2face saw it and requested to see the boy; he gave the boy ₦2m like I was told.

Kola: Wow!

CHAPTER 4

Your Passion, Your Wings

Olu: Ade, I wish I had a sonorous voice like you.

Ade: The last time I checked, you weren't in love with singing; you enjoy reading and writing stories.

Titi: I wonder, oh!

Olu: Yes, that is true, but since musicians are more prominent and make more money, they organize shows, sell their albums, make money from downloads, get royalties from media stations and film producers for using their songs, get invited to parties and even sign endorsement deals, I decided to venture into it.

Ade: Olu, I remember what Titi told me the last time: our gifts and talents are unique and special, which differ from one person to another. It is important that you operate in the area of your interest and passion, or else you will struggle to fit in.

Olu: Well, I still believe one can always develop the ability to sing, even though I might not have the talent or natural ability for it.

Titi: Well, you are right in a way; talent is different from skills, though. Talent is inborn, while skills are acquired. You can develop musical skills, but it is always important that you stay in the place of your natural strength, where you don't need to struggle before you excel. The most important thing is that you are passionate about whatever you do either you have the talents or skills. You don't struggle with what you have passion for because your natural flair does the magic.

Olu: If I may ask, what is passion?

Titi: Passion is a strong feeling of enthusiasm or excitement for something or in doing something. Passion should be one of the major determinants of what you venture into. Your passion should precede the monetary prospects. You see, every business or venture in life has its own challenges; it is the passion you have for it that keeps you going in the face of challenges. Even when you make money but not in the area of your passion, you won't feel fulfilled. I have seen many people who resigned their well-paying jobs to pursue their passion. One of the things that I see with many Nigerians is that they venture into a line of business because others are profiting from it, not necessarily because they have a passion for it. They will see someone making money from frying bean-cake, they too will start, they'll see another running a school, they will also join the trend without discovering what they are passionate about.

Ade: Wow! I remember what Raju said in the film *3 Idiots*, "Make passion your profession and work will be fun" No wonder someone like Kunle Afolayan resigned from a banking job to pursue a career in acting and filmmaking.

Olu: Thanks so much, Titi; I can now see that talent, skills, and passion are necessary ingredients to run a successful business.

CHAPTER 5

A Good Mentor, Your Guiding Light

Ade: Titi, guess what?

Titi: (Smiles) Please what can that be? You know I am terrible at guessing.

Ade: I have discovered my talents and what I am passionate about. I have always loved singing and rapping.

Olu: Sing, let us access you.

Ade: (He coughs to sing but sings off-key) "I believe I can fly; I believe I can touch the sky…"

Olu: (Smiles) That's a good one. You actually have a lovely voice, just like R. Kelly, but you sang off-key.

Titi: I agree with Olu; you have such a lovely voice, but talent is not enough. There are many talented singers yet unknown because they only discovered their talent; they didn't develop it. There are other skills you need to acquire that can help your singing pursuits, such as how to sing along on key, play instruments, sing on stage, modulate your flow with beats, and even dance. These will help you in becoming a good musician.

Olu: That is true. Glad you have started well by discovering your talent; you just have to fine-tune it by acquiring relevant skills.

Titi: You can fine-tune, acquire skills, and develop your talents by getting a mentor, enrolling for training, and observing and watching others. Just like I have grown my business sense through mentorship, mentorship helps you to avoid mistakes, polish your talent and drive your passion.

Ade: I have been hearing the words "mentorship" and "mentor." What do they mean?

Titi: A mentor is an experienced person who teaches, guides or advises a less experienced and often younger person, while mentorship is the process of doing so. Have you heard of Warren Buffet before?

Ade: No.

Titi: What of Bill Gates?

Ade: I know him, the world's richest man before Jeff Bezos and Elon Musk took over.

Olu: Yes, the founder of Microsoft.

Titi: You guys are right; Warren Buffet happened to be a mentor to Bill Gates. In fact, I heard Warren Buffet read a book on investment by Benjamin Graham; this propelled him to travel a very long distance just to learn from him. This culminated in him becoming the richest man for a long time before his mentee, Bill Gates, took over from him. This clearly tells us that having a mentor can actually help you a great deal in life. Isaac Newton once said, "If I can see further, it is because I stand on the shoulders of people who are ahead of me." A mentor would make you see ahead and go further. If you want to be successful in business or any venture, get a mentor!

Olu: I think that is one of the secrets people from the eastern part of Nigeria have when running a successful business.

CHAPTER 6

The Sky is Big Enough

Olu: Ade, how was the Project Fame audition you went for?

Titi: Tell us *nah*... This one, your face is looking like you have just finished crying.

Ade: Chai! I am really discouraged. I didn't qualify.

Olu: *Ah!* Sorry, my guy!

Titi: I am shocked, despite your preparation for that audition. I recall giving you Uncle Asuquo Cohbam's number so he can mentor you, did you contact him?

Ade: Yes. Titi, about that, the preparation period was very short, and he also wasn't in the country at that time. Guys, you needed to see how intimidated I was by those other talents that were there. Men! They were great, with good stage crafts and quality voices. I didn't even stand a chance.

(Kola joins them)

Kola: Ah! Ade, you are here. Sorry, bro, I heard you didn't scale the first stage of the audition. Take heart; it isn't the end of life.

Olu: I learnt that the auditioning for Stardom Nigeria will start soon.

Ade: Leave that matter. I don't think I want to pursue a career in singing anymore. In fact, the music industry is already saturated with both established and upcoming artists.

Titi: Well, they say the sky is big enough for all birds to fly. There is no forever champion; it is only the current champion we have. If Phyno, Simi, Burna Boy and the other new stars allowed the fame and success of artists like Tuface, MI, Brymo, Tiwa and the rest to intimidate them, they wouldn't be where they are today, and they would definitely not be recognized and celebrated today.

Ade: Titi, you don't understand. I don't think my kind can succeed in that industry.

Olu: Never look down on yourself. Are you aware that Adekunle Gold begged Don Jazzy to help him design an ordinary album cover? Today, he has become a sensation in the same music industry just because he didn't give up on himself.

Kola: True. As it is in entertainment, so it is in all fields of life. Others can be there today, but if you don't give up on your dream or allow yourself to be intimidated, your time and chance will surely come.

Titi: You know what? You can create a unique singing style that marks you out from the crowd. Be original, and don't try to imitate someone else. It will certainly draw attention to you. Spread your wings, my friend, and soar like an eagle.

Ade: (Smiling) Wow! You guys are the best! I have gotten new inspiration on how to package and present my music. I will certainly apply online for the Voice Nigeria. See me on your TV screens soon!

Titi, Kola, Ade and Olu: (*Laughed cheerfully.*)

Titi: Yes, oh! This is the Ade we all know!

CHAPTER 7

Believe in Yourself and take up the Challenge

Titi: Guys, who among you would be featured in the stage drama for the end-of-the-year party? *(She starts counting the fingers raised)* Tolu, Bola, Ayo, Kemi, Luke, Atiku, Oluchi, Okiemute, Aloba, Akogun. What about you, Idogbe?

Idogbe: *(She shakes her head because she wasn't acting.)*

Titi: Please, guys, let's all meet at the basketball court during break time. We have less than a month left to plan our storyline and start rehearsals. Idogbe, please wait behind, I'd like to see you. Thanks, guys; we'll see each other later. (*All leave*).

Titi: How are you?

Idogbe: I am fine, thanks.

Titi: I have noticed something about you; despite how brilliant you are, you always shy away whenever people are asked to volunteer to play one role or the other, either in the class debate or quiz. Now, I am wondering why you declined featuring in the school drama since this is just a social event, hope all is well?

Idogbe: All is well; I just don't know how to act.

Titi: What about previous cases of declining to represent your class in quiz or debate competitions? Even when we had the school inter-house sports, you didn't participate in any of the activities.

Idogbe: Titi, I just didn't feel like...

Titi: Idogbe, you are my friend. You don't need to be shy or scared of talking to me. I won't laugh at you, and neither will I tell people about you; it is between the two of us. You see, I am just trying to see if there is any way I can come in and be of help. Very soon, we will be out of school, and we'll have to face life's reality. The earlier we start preparing for the real challenges out there, the better for us.

Idogbe: Thanks for your concern. It's not that I don't feel like participating in all the school and class activities; I just feel like I am not good enough. I feel like if I fail to do well or come first, people will laugh at me, they will mock me, stop associating with me or something like that. Any time I am nominated to represent the class, I decline because it feels like the whole world is on me.

Titi: Thank you for sharing; indeed, a problem shared is half solved. You are not alone in this kind of situation; we all have experienced low self-esteem and a lack of confidence at some point in our lives. Sometimes, we feel we are not good enough and cannot do well; we are afraid of failing, and we don't want to disappoint people so as not to be a laughing stock.

Idogbe: Exactly, that is how I feel.

Titi: Truth be told, as the drama coordinator and head girl, I experience it from time to time. To address this, you must first realize that low/poor self-esteem can make you an easy target for bullies and make you miss out on many life opportunities. To be successful at anything in life, you must be bold and courageous and develop good self-esteem. Ben Carson related his experience in class, how his mates called him blocked head because he started off as a dullard, which adversely affected his self-esteem. However, due to the influence of his mum, he developed a keen interest in reading, which increased his intelligence quotient (IQ). One day, his teacher asked a difficult question in class to which only he could supply the answer, but poor self-esteem and fear of how his classmates would react made him very reluctant to raise his hand. This fight continued within him for a while until he summoned up courage and braced himself for the unknown. All eyes turned towards his direction in shock. Guess what happened?

Idogbe: He got the answer?

Titi: Yes! Just that particular moment changed the entire perspective people had about him. He suddenly became a star amongst his mates, his teacher began to show more interest in him, and his performance in the class soared. He, who used to be relegated, began to take the lead. The resultant effect this had in his life is that it boosted his self-esteem, and he was no longer afraid of people's opinions. But he had to take the first step of conquering his fear. The first step is always the hardest.

Idogbe: That is exactly how I feel. Should I or shouldn't I?

Titi: Yes, that is the feeling. It was not until he decided to give it a try that he was able to conquer his fear. What you don't confront, you cannot conquer. If you are shy, you cannot shine; you don't know what you are capable of doing until you try; the more you try, the more you master it. You just need to conquer your fear, and the surest way is to face it. You see, people will always talk whether you are good or not. Nobody is perfect, including me; I make mistakes a lot, only that I learn from them, and the more I redo an action, the better I become at it. So, my friend, the best way to overcome your fear, timidity and low self-esteem is to dare to try. People will surely laugh at you but see it as a challenge to do better next time. Before your third attempt, you will surely become better and gradually overcome it. He who has never failed has never tried before.

Idogbe: That is true; I pray God helps me.

Titi: Amen. At least one has to try first. Fear of failure or making mistakes prevents many people from trying. It is unknown to them that mistakes or failures are part of the process of succeeding as long as they learn from them. Let me tell you one of the reasons it is important to volunteer or accept responsibility for any task or assignment given to you. My sister once shared with me about some guys in her fellowship who joined the media team, handling cameras, covering services, etc. Can you believe that many of them didn't need their certificate to work after graduation because they have already acquired the knowledge and skills to handle cameras and cover events? They now have their studios and media outfits. Some of them joined the aesthetic/decorating unit, and today, they are now into interior decor, events planning, etc. She also told me of a guy who graduated as a Pharmacist, but today he is fully into the fashion business because back then, on campus, he was assigned to help the fellowship arrange customized vests for anniversaries and special events, from there, he developed an interest and since that time till today he is still into the business, supplying customized wears to churches, schools, fellowships, associations and has his own fashion line now.

Idogbe: Wow! Babe, you are bursting my head here...

Titi: *(Smiles)*. In conclusion, you can never tell how helpful what you are requested to do now can contribute to your future. Knowledge and skills you acquire today have a role to play in the future; they will surely play out. When a child wants to start walking, he first makes mistakes, falls, and stands up again, and before you know it, the muscles become strong enough for him to stand.

Idogbe: I love that illustration; I think I will join you during the break for the drama.

Titi: Beautiful, that is the way to go. See you there.

CHAPTER 8

Maximizing Opportunities

Seyi: Kunle, you used to be a director, filmmaker, and producer, but this one you are now into fashion, ehn, is it everything you want to do? You are a jack of all trades...

Kunle: Master of all...*(chuckles)*... my brother, that's just the way it is.

Seyi: But you didn't go to fashion school, how come?

Kunle: You see, I didn't plan to venture into fashion, but fate happened.

Seyi: Really? So how did it happen?

Kunle: Well, there was a day I was at home with less to do with my filmmaking, so I was checking all these 'kembe' trousers I used to have at home. Sure, you know what kembe is, those big trousers like baggy worn by the Yorubas. So, I decided to trim it down to make it trendier and more fashionable. Behold, my friends loved it. They were interested in knowing who resized it for me; that was how it all started. I called it 'Kunle kembe'.

Seyi: Just like that?

Kunle: Yes, after that, I employed some professional tailors and started using Ankara fabrics for it. I posted some samples on social media, and we started receiving orders from different quarters. Soon, they requested that I give them a top to wear with it, so I started making tops and called it 'Iree'. Then, I started the face cap, and you know the rest. That is how I started my brand, the 'Iree clothing line'.

Seyi: See how you maximized opportunity.

Kunle: That's it, my brother. Can you believe we were featured in the last London Fashion Week and made millions in months?

Seyi: Indeed, you are a jack of all trades and master in all.

Kunle: Thanks, my brother, for the compliments.

CHAPTER 9

In That Problem Lies a Golden Opportunity

(*In what appears to be a continuation of a previous conversation*)

Nuru: I am seriously tired of this country. I wish I could *'japa'*.

Bayo: But why?

Nuru: See, problems are everywhere, and nothing seems to be working in this country anymore. It is like other countries are taking five steps forward while we are taking two steps backwards. Imagine things like corruption, bad leadership, and a poor educational system. Many students can't get admission to the university; many graduates can't get good jobs unless they know somebody in power.

Bayo: Wale, are you not saying anything? You just kept mute from our discussion since.

Wale: Hmm..., I am just reflecting on the happenings around and some of the things my Uncle always tells me and my elder brothers any time he returns from the United States.

Bayo: Can you share with us some of the things he has told you guys, or are they personal?

Wale: My siblings and I have always complained about the situation in this country to my uncle, just like Nuru, with the hope that he would take us along with him next time he travels.

Nuru: So why has he not taken you? If I had someone like that, I would have gone with him because the situation in this country is frustrating.

Wale: Well, he shared a story of two Americans who went to India. When they got there, they saw that the people didn't wear shoes, and one of them started to laugh and make jest of them that they were backward. The other man saw the need of the people as an opportunity to do business, he went back to America, brought shoes to sell, he made huge profit and started his shoe manufacturing company.

Bayo: I am yet to understand the moral of the story.

Wale: My uncle made us understand that where problems exist, business opportunities abound. Unfortunately, many people living in such places don't see the opportunities because complaining and murmuring blindfold them. He gave examples of how the Chinese and the Americans are siphoning the wealth of this nation through their innovations and technology. Imagine, most of these things the Western people sell to us are not needed in their country; they make 'power banks' and sell to us because they saw the problem of power instability; they saw that we have solar energy, so they invent devices that can be powered by solar etc. They make humongous money, which they take to their country. This is why we must think outside the box to find solutions to our problems.

Bayo: For us to be able to find solutions to the problems around us, we need to stop complaining and murmuring and stop being pessimistic about this country.

Nuru: I think you are right in a way, but the situation in the land can be frustrating.

Bayo: I agree with you, but we just have to take advantage of the happenings around us; problems exist for man to solve. When you find the solution to a problem, you can package and commercialize it. You can also use your talent. As for me, though I am studying Computer Science, I would still like to be a motivational speaker because I like talking.

Wale: I feel very happy and fulfilled when I help people solve their problems. This country has power problems, corruption issues, agricultural and food problems, and insecurity problems, and the masses are suffering; so, since I like politics, I may end up being part of the policymakers so one can find better ways to solve them.

Nuhu: You guys are correct; I remember while growing up, I found it hard to recite the multiplication table until my aunt got a cassette where the multiplication table was recorded in the form of a song; reciting times table became easy and pleasurable to me and many others who found it hard. I am pretty sure those who did this made money from selling the product to us.

Bayo: Indeed, problems are loaded with lots of business opportunities. The more the problem, the more the opportunities. Entrepreneurs rejoice at problems because that is their stepping stone to greatness.

CHAPTER 10

Think Outside That Box

Wale: Wow! Gboyega, where have you been? I can't believe my eyes. This can't be true...

Gboyega: It is true, it is me. It has been ages...

Wale: Yes, ever since we left secondary school four years ago.

Gboyega: So, how have you been? Where are you now?

Wale: Well, I am in 400 level at the Ladoke Akintola University of Technology, studying Computer Science; what about you?

Gboyega: Well, I am still seeking admission into the university. I am preparing for the next JAMB; I had issues with the CBT in the last exams.

Wale: Hmmm, let me see what I can do... Okay, I will talk to my friend so that we can design an app that will have JAMB's past questions and their solutions for you, which will serve as a model for you to prepare for CBT exams.

Gboyega: That is thoughtful of you.

(Wale gets to school and calls his friend Bayo, who is also a programmer like him)

Wale: Bayo, please, there is a project I would like you to assist me with; there is this secondary school friend of mine who has been having issues with JAMB, so I want us to help him develop an app that can have JAMB pass questions with their solutions and a model that will prepare him for CBT exams.

Bayo: That will be time-consuming, but let us get it done.

Wale: Come to think of it. It just dawned on me that it is not only Gboyega who will be in this situation; there are other students who also have issues with JAMB, for which I believe this app can be useful.

Bayo: You are very correct.

(They developed the app and it worked)

Bayo: Thank God you were willing to help your friend with this app; see how far it has taken us now. We have won awards in the country and even in South Africa just because of our innovations inspired by what we did for your friend; the app is now used all over the country.

Wale: My friend, I return the praise to God; thank God for the inspiration to start www.pass.ng. I have seen the importance of being willing to help people out, which has given me the opportunity to do business.

CHAPTER 11

Be the Solution Plug

Lolu: Why is it that you are always going about with your charger?

Nuhu: There has been no power supply in my area for the past three weeks since a thunderstorm affected our transformer.

Lolu: So for the past three weeks, they have not been able to fix it?

Nuhu: *For where?* Except they do that today.

Tayo: See, Ghana, our neighbouring country, has a steady power supply. The country is so well organized. Also, see South Africa; they generate 40,000KWA of power while the so-called giant of Africa cannot boast of 10,000KWA.

Bayo: Tayo! Lolu! Are you guys not 400-level Physics students? Why can't you look inward to proffer a solution to the power problem in your immediate environment by using the resources around you, such as solar, water, and fossil waste? Must you always blame the government?

Lolu: Bayo, we are not even well equipped as students to embark on such capital-intensive projects. Governments in other countries have created an environment that enables students to exercise their creativity. They even make funds available to support their inventions. But it isn't so in this country.

Nuhu: I tire oh!

Bayo: Is it only problems and negativity you guys see? You see, that is why many Nigerians are poor. They are always complaining and lamenting instead of being solution-driven. We are good at identifying problems but not the solution. Don't you know that when you solve a problem, you become a celebrity and surely have returns for it? That is why I was motivated to join hands with Wale to create that JAMB app that everyone is talking about today. This is also why foreigners are still coming here despite how beautiful their country is and how 'bad' ours is. They see solutions to our problems, they make solutions available, we pay for the solutions, and they take our money to their country. They don't need rechargeable fans, generators, power banks and so on; we need them. We keep complaining while they keep feeding on us. So, my conclusion is this: instead of always complaining, lamenting, trading blame, and giving excuses, let us seek solutions to the problems around us; let us ponder on how we can proffer solutions to the problems around us; this is what entrepreneurship is about. The more problems we solve, the more life becomes bearable for the people and the more they appreciate our work both in cash and in kind.

Lolu: I think you are right. I remember the last time I was in Lagos, there was heavy downpour, people found it hard to pass a place because of the flood, some guys came together to find a way of helping people cross by collecting a token. We need to look beyond the problems to see the solutions.

Tayo: *(Thinking aloud)* I have finally found a project topic. I will use my acquired knowledge to create a solar inverter and will make money from it, too. You two will be my first customers.

Bayo: That's great, as long as you sell at a discounted rate to us because we motivated you.

Innovation – The Key

John: Hey Bola! What is this that you are drinking? I am sure it is new in town because I have never seen it before.

Bola: Of course, it is the newest Cola drink in town, and believe me, the taste is great!

Lolu: Wow! Bola, my brother, you are very correct; the taste is refreshingly different from the existing ones. But do you know I drank it because the bottle is so attractive?

Peter: Please, what's the hype about? All I know is that all of them are still Cola drinks because they are made from Cola.

John: My dear doubting Peter, that is where innovation in business comes into play, my friend.

Peter: I laugh in innovation! This is pure copycat!

John: Yes, innovation is the creative ability to alter or to change into something new. That is to say, doing something in a new way using new approaches or making something already in existence better.

Lolu: Gbam! Simply put, I can take an existing idea, improve on it and repackage it, or I can get more creative and do something completely new and different.

Bola: I agree with you; one can always repackage already existing products into a new one by making them more appealing and attractive. One can always add value to the content of an already existing product to taste sweeter, more nutritious and more beneficial. One can always improve the way something works to make it more effective and less stressful to use. One can always find better ways of doing things to make them cheaper, more affordable, more efficient and more effective. Innovation is all about finding ways to improve a product so that customers and consumers enjoy more value and satisfaction for their money.

John: You are right; most of the things that are new today have always existed; some persons simply repackaged them and added more value to them. They came up with new and better ways of offering the same services or packaging a product to save people's time, energy and resources.

Bola: What you can call rebranding, modification or repackaging.

John: Exactly! I heard the story of how Goffried Williams Leibniz improved the Pascaline invented by Blaise Pascal. Pascaline had some limitations, but he improved on them.

Bola: Yes, even Cola-Cola, Nigerian Breweries Plc. have changed the bottles of their products many times to look handier and appealing to their customers.

Peter: Hmmm...You guys are very right, I remember in my primary school, we made use of blackboard, now we are using white board while some schools are already using digital or electronic board. People are just innovating new ways of doing things.

John: My dad once showed me the first GSM he used, the Nokia 3310- big and heavy yet couldn't browse; it was mainly used for calls and SMS. See how phones have evolved; we now have iPhones and Android phones that can do many things at the same time because some people thought of ways to improve telecommunications technology. I am sure you are aware that some countries are planning to replace cars powered by fuel with vehicles that will run on solar power, water and other elements.

Bola: Indeed, the world is dynamic; one has to be innovative to be an entrepreneur and stay in business. Think of new ways of doing things, think of new ways of packaging already existing things to make them more durable and easier to use for users; like some persons are now packaging beans flour and potato flour in sachets, saving consumers stress of removing the chaff and peeling, you don't need to go about with cash as ATM, POS are now available to ease the risk of carrying cash about. In fact, so many innovations are just taking place.

Lolu: But guys, you know you can be innovative with your talent too. Take Kenny Blaq, the standup comedian. Instead of doing same talk and laugh like others, he does his own comedy using people's songs and making them funny.

Peter: I think we too have to think of new ways of doing business, adding value to already existing products, rendering services, and presenting our talents in a better way...

CHAPTER 13

Add Value, Raise Your worth

James: Daddy, Uncle Nuru and his friends were discussing something outside, but I didn't understand. Why is it that many Nigerians want to travel to America, Canada, Europe and the like?

Daddy: It is because of our economic condition. You see, the Western world's economy is more developed than ours.

James: Dad, I still don't seem to understand, sir.

Daddy: My son, you see, economy means the process or system by which goods and services are produced, sold and bought in a country. In the Western world, they have a high level of technology that allows goods to be produced at faster, easier, and cheaper rates than here in Nigeria. Services can be accessed and provided more easily in all areas than here. This is why they have good roads, good health facilities, a good educational system, employment opportunities, good policing and security apparatus, a favourable business environment, good weapons of war, good machinery and equipment for production, and a digitalized and mechanized farming system. I mean, things are working out there.

James: Dad, but Nigeria is more endowed than the countries of the world because of the mineral and natural resources we have here; we have good arable lands for farming, crude oil, wonderful weather conditions, so many resources under the earth as well as great manpower in terms of human capital but why are things not working well in this country?

Daddy: You are right, my son. Nature has blessed us tremendously, but one major difference between Nigeria and other developed nations is in the area of value addition.

James: Value addition, how?

Daddy: Let me explain it like this: Nigeria is blessed with crude oil, but we cannot use it in its raw form; it has to be refined to get premium motor spirit (PMS), gas, aviation fuel and other products but unfortunately, we don't have functioning refineries which means we have to import fuel to meet our local consumption. In the world market, a barrel of crude oil is sold for less than $65, but refined oil is sold at a higher rate, sometimes double the cost of crude oil. So, who do you think makes more money?

James: The countries that sell refined products.

Daddy: Yes, because refined products are more expensive than crude products/raw materials. This is what is called value addition. Developed countries are able to make more money than underdeveloped or developing countries because they add value to products and sell at higher prices to developing countries that only generate the raw materials. Do you know a farmer who plants and harvests cassava can never make money like someone who refines the cassava to make cassava flour, garri and the rest for sale?

James: Wow! That is why foreign countries make more money and are able to develop their countries; they refine cocoa into cocoa drinks, chocolate, biscuits, candies and so on.

Daddy: Yes, that is why those who add value to farm produce make more money than the farmers who produce them because of the value addition. It is not enough to generate raw materials; one must also think about how to convert them to refined goods.

James: I see...

Daddy: You see, in life, it is your value that determines your worth. The more value you add to a product, the higher the price and the more money you make on it. The more value you add to yourself and what you offer, the higher your worth. One should always think of ways to add more value to already existing goods or ways of doing things so that the needs of the consumer would be met directly without the need for them to work on it again. This is the secret to why Nigerians are running out of the country. The Western world keeps adding value to already existing products and developing ways of doing things better, and that is why life is much more comfortable, and opportunities abound there.

James: Thanks so much, Dad. I have really learned a lot.

Daddy: You're welcome, my son; I'm sure you will reason along this line; let us go and meet others at the dining table for dinner.

CHAPTER 14

Content Before Packaging

John: Bola! Peter! Look at this news update I just read online now!

Peter: (*Reads it out*) "Coca-Cola retrieved a particular batch of Eva water from circulation". But why would they do that?

Bola: Oh! That? It's been in circulation since yesterday. That is the problem: when they ask you to listen to the news, you will not, but you'll focus all your attention on movies, entertainment stories, and online celebrity gossips.. Listen to the news and stay current.

Peter: You still haven't answered the question.

Bola: Well, they discovered it could be harmful to human health if consumed.

Peter: Are you for real?

Bola: Yes, of course, it was on 9 o'clock network news.

John: One has to be careful with what one consumes.

Bola: Well, I guess the quality control didn't certify and approve it for distribution. Normally, there is a quality control department in any manufacturing company that makes sure the product meets all the necessary requirements by NAFDAC, SON and other agencies before distributing them all over; if NAFDAC should discover any product not meeting the requirements, they have the power to retrieve such products from circulation and can even sue or fine the manufacturing company.

Peter: Is it that serious?

John: Yes, there was a time when a particular brand of noodles, as well as one particular brand of insecticide, were called back from circulation so that they would not harm innocent consumers. This is why the contents should be scrutinized before packaging. There was a time when a man made millions of naira from a mineral company when he discovered an insect inside a bottle of a soft drink. So, before you package your product for consumption, it is important you verify and certify your product. People can buy your product the first time because of the container that looks beautiful and appealing, but they will only buy it again because of the content.

Peter: That is deep; I can now see how it relates to business. One should make sure the value is in place before the packaging. Content should have more priority than the container.

Bola: Exactly my point. Do you know that it is not only applicable to tangible products?

Peter: Really? What do you mean?

Bola: It is applicable to all we do as humans. For example, it is not only the outfit, makeup, and paparazzi that we look out for in our favourite musicians. It is their song lyrics, the melody, the quality of their voice, their passion and their personality that eventually make us fans.

Peter: (*Laughs*) Just like how our ladies nowadays wear wigs, heavy makeup, and skimpy clothes to attract guys, forgetting that the outward appearance (container) can only attract a guy, but it is their content (character and intelligence) that will keep him.

John: We should think of the value people will derive from our product before we garnish, brand or package it because if you want to keep your customers and encourage more patronage, you should think about value first. Don't sell a product you are not sure of its value to the people.

CHAPTER 15

Packaging Enhances Value

Cynthia: Sandra, you can make up for Africa.

Sandra: Before *nko*? As an original, beautiful lady that I am, I must always look good.

Cynthia: *I hear you.*

Peter: Girls! May God help you people *oh*! Remember, you are not to judge a book by its cover.

Sandra: Meaning?

Peter: It is not your physical look that determines who you are. You can't keep a man by your outlook but by your character.

Sandra: I am not disputing that, but Oga Peter, tell me, what is the very first thing that attracts you as a guy to a lady? Is it her character?

Cynthia: Well, it is her appearance.

Sandra: Oh, oh... have you forgotten that the way you dress is the way you will be addressed? You see, one must look beautiful on the outside. I am not dressing because I want to impress any man, but one thing I have realized is that the container must be appealing and attractive. As much as I must work on my character, I must also make sure I look good. The first thing a man will see is the physical look before the character, or will it be the character he will see from afar that will attract him? So, as much as I am working on my character to keep him, I must also work on my physical appearance to attract him.

Peter: You have a point there.

Cynthia: You see, this is applicable to business. Customers will keep patronizing you because of the value they derive from the product you produce or sell and the services you render, but they will first come to you or buy your product because of the way you attract them and appeal to their emotions. You know, humans are naturally attracted to what they see. Our emotions easily connect to our five senses: what we see, what we hear, what we feel, what we touch and what we taste. So, we should always make the outlook appealing to potential and established customers and consumers. Remember, first impressions last for long. You see, packaging always enhances value.

Sandra: Cynthia, you are very correct. *(Peter started going)* Let me finish with the process of packaging my container.

CHAPTER 16

Know Your Product (KYP)

Ayo: Hello, young girl; what are you selling?

Seller: Good afternoon. I am selling walnuts.

Ayo: Walnuts? What is that? I have never heard of or seen it before. What are its benefits?

Seller: It is very good for the body's system and is nutritious and medicinal.

Ayo: Really? Can you tell me how medicinal it is?

Seller: It is rich in antioxidants (a substance added to food and other products to prevent harmful chemical reactions in which oxygen is combined with the substance), it prevents inflammation (a condition in which a part of your body becomes red, swollen and hurtful), it promotes a healthy gut, it reduces the risk of some cancers, it supports weight control, it helps to manage type II diabetes and lowers the risk, it helps lower blood pressure and many more.

Ayo: Wow! Are you kidding me? I am really thrilled by the knowledge you have about your product... but how come you know much about walnuts?

Seller: I heard my mum talk about it, and I also Googled it to get more information about it.

Ayo: I am highly impressed; I would like to buy ₦500 worth of walnuts.

Seller: With all pleasure, I have added 2 extra as your *jara* (bonus).

Ayo: Take this ₦1000 and keep the change.

Seller: Thank you so much.

Ayo: You are welcome.

(Ayo gets home to inform his mum about his encounter with the walnut seller)

Ayo: Good afternoon ma.

Ayo's mum: My son, you are welcome; how was school today?

Ayo: It was fine. I bought this on my way home; it is called walnuts.

Mum: Yes, it is very nutritious and medicinal.

Ayo: Mum, you can't believe the seller told me many things about it today. She said it is a good source of antioxidants, and it also prevents cancer.

Mum: That's very good of her; it shows she knows her product very well and can guide her customers. You see, in business, it is good to know your products; it helps you to speak boldly, assuredly and confidently about them, which helps in convincing your potential customers. I remember the story of a young man, even though he was a graduate, who ended up selling a brand of malt drink on the highway; on a faithful day, the CEO of the company parked to ask him about the malt he was selling, the man said so many good things about it. This impressed the CEO, who gave him his card and asked him to see him in his office; when he got there, he made him the marketing manager.

Ayo: Wow! It is indeed good to have knowledge of what you sell and how it can add value to potential customers' success in business. I believe this will help you market your product well, even when one is an introvert.

Mum: Exactly! Knowing your products and how they can be beneficial to potential customers serves as a platform you can leverage, even if you are a shy person. When you speak to two or more people, you become confident and surprisingly become an expert marketer. Go and freshen up, your lunch is ready.

CHAPTER 17

Raising Capital for Your Business

Chidi: You are looking so unhappy this morning.

Kosini: Well, you are right; ever since our last discussion on starting our own business, an idea has dropped on my mind, but all my efforts to source the money needed to start have been in vain. It seems nobody wants to help me out. Yours has kicked off already.

Chidi: Oh, you are referring to the capital to start the business. I think you are not the only one in such a situation; there are many youths who complain that they have great business ideas but no capital to finance them.

Kosini: Okay. The money needed to start a business is called capital?

Chidi: Yes, the money and resources needed to start or manage a business to ensure its growth is called capital. I too had that challenge when I wanted to start mine.

Kosini: So, how were you able to solve the problem?

Chidi: Let me ask you, do you have any savings?

Kosini: Well, I tried to, but I kept dipping my hands into it when any need arose.

Chidi: There are many places one can source capital, but it is always good to have personal savings. This will motivate those who want to support, partner or invest in your idea. They will see that you are really serious. Even banks and other financial institutions want to know if you have part of the money needed before giving you a loan.

Kosini: Hmmm, I need to start saving again then, but where will I really get the money to save? Is it from the meager pocket money that dad gives me?

Chidi: Well, don't despise the days of little beginning. A drop of water, they say, makes the mighty ocean. Oluwatoyosi Alade, in his book *Small Contains All*, made me realize that the small you think you have can actually be all you need. No matter how little, just start saving. What you will save at the end may just be 3/10 of the total amount needed for the business, but it is good to save. Save money given to you by your parents, uncles, and parents' friends, and you can also look for side jobs to do, like doing tutorials for your friends in those subjects you are good at. I am pretty sure not less than ₦500 passes through your hand in a week.

Kosini: Hmmm, you are right; in some weeks, I could make more than that, though. But where can I keep my money so as not to spend it?

Chidi: You can have a contribution group in your school, you can make use of a piggy bank or give to a trusted teacher who you can entrust with your money. In my case, we have a contribution group in my class, and we keep our money with Mr. Isaiah, who has been gracious enough not to touch it. The last time I tried saving at home, my mum collected everything in the guise of borrowing to return it.

Kosini: I can relate to that.

Chidi: You might also share your idea with someone you trust, thereby reducing the burden of sourcing the capital alone. You can also start small with the little money you have and manage it well to grow; you can also use the power of integrity.

Kosini: How can one start a business with integrity?

Chidi: Well, with integrity, you can get goods on credit from the supplier, sell, make your profit and pay for the goods to the supplier. You can also act as an agent by making a deal with the supplier that gives you a commission at the end of the day.

Kosini: Thanks, friend; you have actually opened my mind to some ways I can go about it. Indeed, a problem shared is half solved.

Chidi: You are welcome. Don't ever allow the fear of where you will get capital to stop you from dreaming. Do you know that the passion for your business can get to a point where it will attract investors and make them buy into your ideas?

Bukola: I couldn't help but listen to your conversation. Can I add something?

Chidi: Yes, please do. No man is an island of knowledge.

Bukola: Okay. Another way you can raise capital is to make a list of your gifts/talents and match them with the names of individuals or groups of people who need and will pay for them. Or you can volunteer your time and service for a token.

Kosini: Please expatiate on the latter.

Bukola: Okay. Let me use this example. The youths in my church wanted to organize a party and conference and needed to raise money, so they devised a means. One Sunday morning, while the service was on, they mobilized themselves and washed all the cars in the church; by the time the congregants came out, they were shocked. They seized the opportunity to inform them of the intending programme and guess what? They received more than enough because the people were highly impressed by this service.

Kosini: Wow! I will do as advised. Thanks guys!

CHAPTER 18

Start Small

Bukola: Kossy! Kossy! How far?

Kosini: I am just there, oh, my sister.

Bukola: So, have you decided on when you want to start your business now? Or have you started already?

Kosini: Start fire! I have yet to start. Though I am very confident that it is a very good and viable business idea, I am still waiting for money to start it.

Bukola: But you told me the last time that you had already saved up some money. Have you spent the money again?

Kosini: Not at all. I have saved ₦15,000, but I want to start the business with ₦50,000.

Bukola: I can see you want to start in a big way.

Kosini: Something like that.

Bukola: Wow! That is beautiful; as much as I support starting big, I will not neglect the power of starting small. Rome wasn't built in a day like they always say. If one has the means to start big, no problem, but from records, most successful businesses started small and grew to be great. An example is Bill Gates and his partner, who both started small. Also, Steve Jobs and his partner started in the Garage; some even started in their bedroom. All I am just saying is you might as well start with the capital you have now so you gain more experience in the business. Start small and see it grow.

Kosini: I think you are right in a way because I have seen someone doing the exact thing I have in mind.

Bukola: Hmmm, that is another thing that procrastination causes. Ideas keep flying every time; those who embrace them first and run with them flourish from them. It is not good to delay in getting things done. It is never too early to start; you just have to strategize and package your own in a different or unique way, and you will surely have your own market share.

Kosini: I quite agree with you. I remember we were among the pioneering students of our school; only 25 of us started the school. Then we had just six full-time teachers and only a few classrooms, but now, we have JSS1-SSS2 with new structures in place; we have all the labs, an ICT room, more than 500 students and 45 teachers excluding the non-teaching staff. Indeed, it is never wrong to start small if one can maintain focus, determination and consistency.

Bukola: Exactly my point! Lastly, don't jettison an idea because it looks small. Don't take some relationships for granted because the people seem to have little or nothing to offer you.

Kosini: Without any further ado, it's high time I started my business.

CHAPTER 19

Sacrifice and Self-Denial

Chidi: Chisom! Chisom! Chisom!

Chisom: Yes, big brother.

Chidi: How many times did I call you?

Chisom: Three times.

Chidi: You have been saying you wanted to start a business before you get to your final year.

Chisom: *Yes ooo*, nothing can change that plan. I want to be like you; I know you started your business in your final year, and it is really doing well, so I want to break your record.

Chidi: So, how far have you gone with the plan? In fact, do you even have a business plan? And if I may ask, how much have you saved?

Chisom: Well bro, to answer your plenty questions. Number 1, I don't have a concrete plan yet. Number 2, I still have two years to graduate. Number 3, I don't have the luxury of time to plan as you well know, I still have my books to concentrate on and Number 4, I have more pressing financial needs now, so I don't have any savings for any business now.

Chidi: Ah! You see, that's the point! Before you know it, you will be in your final year and out of school, by then my dear baby brother, you will still be financially dependent on Dad, Mum and myself.

Chisom: Are you cursing me?

Chidi: Curse? Never! You see, many people have beautiful dreams and great aspirations, but they fail to realize that it takes sacrifice to achieve their goals, dreams and aspirations. The great business empire you dream about comes your way day by day, bit by bit today. It is like building a skyscraper; you start by laying block on block till you finally complete it. I need to advise you as a brother. Thank God you said you want to break my record.

Chisom: Hmmm! Yes, of course!

Chidi: But you may not be able to do so if you keep spending your money on Domino pizza, Cold stone Ice cream or Tantalizer Sharwarma as you do almost on a daily basis as *Aberuagba pikin* of that TV program *My siblings and I*. See your expensive designer clothes and shoes. Your wristwatch alone can buy 100 blocks to build a house.

Chisom: Ahan! My brother! There is a Yoruba adage that says, *"Nkan ti eye ba je ni oma gbe fo"* (It is what birds eat that they use to fly). It is an inner strength that strengthens us.

Chidi: Well, I am not disputing that one has to eat well and look good, but it is wise to cut down on one's excesses. You can cut your spending to save for your business. To succeed in business or any venture in life, one must be disciplined and ready to make sacrifices. I remember when I was in 100 Level, I was given fifteen thousand naira per month for my upkeep; I ensured that I saved at least five thousand naira every month from my first year. By the time I got to my third year, I already had a substantial amount to start my business. Mum and Uncle Emeka saw this, and it motivated them to help me complete the amount needed. Look at you, Mum gives you twenty-five thousand naira every month, not to mention all the cash our uncles and aunties give you as per the last born that you are, yet you have no savings. Maybe you have forgotten we don't use the ten fingers to eat.

Chisom: Hmmm!

Chidi: You claim there is no time to plan your business, yet you have time to go to viewing centres to watch football matches, go to clubs and attend shows. When I was in my first year, I took time to study the environment, the trends on campus, the common needs of students and ways of solving them. By the time I was in year two, I was already perfecting my plans, and I finally launched in my 3rd year, second semester. Well, I am not saying you should be like me; I am not saying you shouldn't have time for recreation and relaxation, but you should create time for things that are profitable to you. Doing great things is not always achieved on a platter of gold; you have to work hard and be willing to go the extra mile. The truth is many people wish for greatness, but only a few are ready to pay the price. For every prize to be won, there is always a price to pay. If wishes were horses, beggars might ride. You need to stop this wishful thinking and put concrete actions in place. I am sure you know everybody wants to finish with a First class grade, but you know those who do always go the extra mile. So is business; you must be ready to sacrifice your time, resources, sleep, pleasure and comfort, at least at the beginning.

Chisom: Hmmm!

Chidi: That's it, my brother. I once heard Dangote say, *"The passion for my business makes me sleep for 4 hours"*. Dr Oyedepo once said he worked all day on a particular day that he forgot he hadn't had breakfast when he was not on a fast. You and your friend - Femi keep buying liabilities instead of investing them in assets; assets bring you money in return, while liabilities always take from you.

Chisom: Big brother, it is not easy to be in business.

Chidi: Well, so is every other endeavour; sacrifice is required to be successful in life, except if one wants to be a failure or a nonentity.

Chisom: Thanks, big brother, for sharing some of your secrets with me; I will surely adjust and make amends.

Chidi: You're welcome.

CHAPTER 20

Assets and Liabilities

Chisom: My G, the biggest boy on Campus, Femi, my guy!

Femi: Yes, oh! What's up, Chiboy? Thank God it's Friday! We are going to paint the town red tonight!

Chisom: My guy, I don't think I will be joining you.

Femi: Why? (*Asked with a contoured face*) You that like enjoyment more than life.

Chisom: I am learning to set my priorities right.

Femi: But it is just one day, and today is the right day to take a well-deserving break. Besides, all the big boys and big girls on Campus will be at the Bush Bar and Club, so my dear, you can't afford to miss it.

Chisom: No, bro. I need to dedicate more time to planning my business, and today is just right for it. Besides, I have started saving for my business and don't have money to throw around again.

Femi: Oh, is that why you stopped hanging out with us and buying your regulars like pizza and the rest? Recall our mantra: *"It is what the bird eats that it flies with"*.

Chisom: Yes. I don't want to spend my money on liabilities again; I'd rather spend on assets.

Femi: What do you mean by that? So, what are you saying in essence?

Chisom: You see, I know nobody wants to be wretched in life, but the fact is, many people don't know what it takes to be rich. One of the keys to being rich is to spend more money on assets and less money on liabilities.

Femi: Did I hear you say assets and liabilities?

Chisom: Yes. You see many people, including adults, make that mistake; the right thing to do is to invest in assets and then use the returns to finance their liabilities.

Femi: Hmm...Continue

Chisom: Assets are anything of value that a man owns and can bring money to him, while liability is what an individual owes and must be returned or paid. This means that assets add to you while liability takes from you. For example, this party or club you said you are going to, is it not money you are going to spend there? What value will it add to you? It will only consume your time and resources.

Femi: Hmm...Continue.

Chisom: Let me use this phone as an example. Do you know this phone can function as an asset or as a liability If it is used productively? When we use it for online business, business promotions, contacting customers, training and development of oneself, and getting information about life opportunities, then it is an asset. But if the same phone is used only for chatting, watching entertainment stories, calling friends and families and gossiping without bringing money to you or adding value to you, it is a liability because you have to keep buying data and call cards.

Femi: Hmm! It is just like a car; it can serve as an asset and a liability depending on its usage.

Chisom: Exactly my point. If the car is used for business purposes or aids in one's work that brings money or helps one to develop his capacity to become more productive, it is an asset. If the car is not used for economic purposes or to help you meet your job needs, it is a liability because you need to fuel it and pay for the servicing and maintenance. So, always separate assets from liabilities; before you spend money on anything, make sure you determine if that thing is an asset or liability.

Femi: It is not easy, but I quite agree with you; if I want to spend on anything, I should first think about how it can be beneficial to me, I should always choose assets above comfort, the proceeds from the assets can later buy me the comfort.

Chisom: That's the best way to enjoy life, my brother.

Femi: But Chisom, what influenced this sudden change in you that you are now talking like a finance expert?

Chisom: Hmm! It was the conversation I had with my elder brother - Chidi, who is a business tycoon, that changed my thinking pattern.

CHAPTER 21

Venture Capitalists

Chidi: Bukky, how are you doing today?

Bukola: I am very fine, thank you. You?

Chidi: I am fine too. I am happy for Kossy; she has finally started the much-awaited business.

Bukola: You can say that again. I am happier because the business is doing great, just as she predicted. I am even on my way to her shop. Would you mind joining me? Thank God you have salespersons now to help you run your business.

Chidi: All thanks to God. At least I have more hands to help with the sales as the business keeps growing. I couldn't handle it all by myself anymore.

Bukola: Wow! Thank God. If that is the case, let's go and see Kossy.

Kosini: Bukola! Welcome! Oh, you came with Chidi? Just who I have been yearning to see but there has been no time. Chidi, how are you?

Chidi: I am fine. I can see your business is doing well.

Kosini: Yes, it's actually a laudable, viable and extremely profitable business. I am even thinking of making it bigger. The idea is for me to add delivery services to it so customers can place orders online, and my dispatch riders will go and deliver. But this will require more capital.

Bukola: Great! But have you drawn the business plan for this new idea of yours?

Kosini: I have done that already. The estimated take off cost is ₦500,000 and I only have ₦220,000.

Chidi: Have you considered going into partnership or getting a venture capitalist?

Kosini: As for partnerships, I have never thought of that, but what do you mean by venture capitalist?

Chidi: A venture capitalist is an investor who is ready to invest in a business idea for an agreed interest over time, while venture capital is the money that a venture capitalist is ready to invest in the business idea. Venture capitalist studies the prospects of the business, and if they see it viable enough, they invest their money in it.

Kosini: I wouldn't mind that; I think I like that idea, but where do I get to see them? And what do they look for?

Bukola: Well, they are everywhere; it is just to have what they are looking out for. The basic things they look for are: the competence and experience of the manager of the business, the value customers stand to enjoy and how to capture them, clear cut analysis of likely competitors and how to beat them, clear evaluation of risks and opportunities and how they will recoup their money.

Chidi: Wait, ladies, let me see your business plan and income analysis to see how viable this is. I think I am interested in investing in this your business idea.

Kosini: Really? Wow! I feel so happy! You have made my day.

CHAPTER 22

Profits in Business

Bola: My friend, how is your business?

Kola: It is just there. I am even thinking of taking a break from it.

Bola: But why?

Kola: I don't seem to be making a profit from this business, which is against the goal of setting a business up.

Bola: How do you know if you are making a profit or not?

Kola: When the money I make is greater than the money spent. That is, when my income is greater than my expenses, when the selling price is greater than the cost price. For example. If I bought a candy bar at ₦500 and sold it at ₦700, the selling price is ₦700 while the cost price is ₦500, the profit is ₦200

Bola: That makes ₦200 profit. I thought you said the business is not profitable.

Kola: Yes, you see, that ₦200 is the gross profit; there are other expenses that have to be deducted from it to get the net profit. For example, if the transportation cost of moving the goods is ₦50, the cost of carriage is ₦50, and the cost for sales boy wages is ₦50, then I end up having only ₦50, which is the net profit.

Bola: I see. So, will gross profit minus expenses give net profit?

Kola: Yes.

Bola: How come you only made a gross profit of ₦200 from the whole packs?

Kola: Well, I think I made mistakes. I gave out some candy bars without accounting for them, and I withdrew parts of the money without taking a record.

Bola: This means you would have made a higher gross profit if you accounted for the personal withdrawal and gifted out candy bars.

Kola: Absolutely, yes. Next time, I will make a proper recording of every single item to determine how much profit I make. I will not throw in the towel; I now know where the problems lie.

CHAPTER 23

Accountability/Proper Bookkeeping

Bola: My friend, you are looking so happy this morning.

Kola: Yes, you can say that again. Well, I am pretty sure you are wondering why. The reason is not far-fetched. I am beginning to record significant profits in my business.

Bola: Oh, I am so happy for you. So, you are making tremendous profits this time around?

Kola: You see, after our last discussion, I decided to make adjustments to how I run my business. I started keeping proper records of the operations of my business, including goods I bought, goods I sold, those who paid and those who bought on credit. This really helped me monitor the growth of my business, determine the gross profit and net profit, and compare changes in my business from time to time. I also believe this will help me by the time my business is registered, and I will need to pay taxes and attract investors.

Bola: Wow! You made me see the importance of keeping proper books in business.

Kola: Yes, one keeps learning on the job. Unlike before, I wasn't accountable for my biscuits and sweets business. I could just give people things for free without recording or paying for them; I now do. I have now separated my business from me. If I take anything for personal use or give it to someone, I make sure I pay for it, and I return any money I quickly borrowed from the business.

Bola: Hmmm! I think you just made a very salient point on why many businesses fail in Nigeria. The owners fail to separate their personal money from that of their business. I remember when we went to greet Grandma; she would just give us sweets and biscuits from her shop for free; I am sure she didn't pay back the money. My sister, selling foodstuff, will pack food to give to Mum any time I stop by her shop.

Kola: You are very right; many of us are generous that we give people part of what we sell, thinking we are being kind, not knowing we are eating our business capital. What could have been used to grow the business is given out. There is nothing wrong with being generous, but we either give out of the profit we have made or pay from our purse what we give. This is how philanthropic acts will not affect the growth of our business.

Bola: You are right. Another area in which many people make mistakes is taking part of the capital or profit for personal use without returning it.

Kola: In fact, it has happened to me too many times; they call it drawings. Thank God, I have learnt my lessons; anytime I withdraw for personal use, I make sure I write it down and as soon as I get cash somewhere, I return it.

Bola: You are really learning on the job.

Kola: You can say that again.

CHAPTER 24

Beware of Credit Sales

Titi: Idowu, you are here. Let's go and see Kola in his shop. I told Bola I would meet him there.

Idowu: Okay. Let's go since I am not engaged now.

Titi: Ah! What about your business?

Idowu: Which business?

Titi: Thought you started the same business with Kola? Or are you not buying and selling sweets and biscuits again?

Idowu: Business that has long been forgotten.

Titi: How come? But you did great in advertising your business. Our mates patronized you a lot; you used to sell close to 50 pieces in a day.

Bola: Oh! Here she is. Idowu, why aren't you in your place of business, and why are you looking so downcast?

Titi: Hmmm! Bola, thanks for waiting for me here. Idowu and I were just discussing his business.

Kola: Oh! What about it?

Titi: His business has packed up.

Kola: What happened, Idowu? You were my major competitor.

Idowu: Yes, I was just telling Titi on our way here that I used to sell a lot on a daily basis, but that was because I was selling on a credit basis. Many of my classmates collected sweets and biscuits with the promise of paying later, only for them to default and come up with excuses.

Kola: Ah! You mean you sold all your sweets and biscuits to the people on credit?

Idowu: Yes, what a great regret; it is a big lesson to me.

Bola: Credit sales most times lead to bad debt.

Idowu: What is bad debt?

Titi: Debt that cannot be recovered. You see, in my mum's shop, she boldly wrote it in a conspicuous place: 'No credit today, come tomorrow'. Even though credit sales have its own advantage of higher profit margin sometimes, but it is better to sell on cash basis to people you cannot trust. If you don't have the courage to ask for your money or means to get your money back, don't sell on credit.

Idowu: That is exactly what happened to me. I don't like embarrassing people by asking them for money they owe me.

Bola: That means you are not wired to be selling on credit; you see, it is easier for people to collect things from you on credit, but when the time comes to pay, they start acting funny. If you cannot be firm and courageous, your money is gone. Credit sales can affect the growth of your business because your capital will be tied in the hands of the debtors who buy goods on credit. Well, it is a lesson; don't let that discourage you from doing business. Just make sure you avoid selling on credit to people you can't vouch for or people you will find it difficult to ask for your money from.

Idowu: Thank you, my friends. I am encouraged, and I think I will start all over again.

Kola: I have also learnt another lesson here. Idowu, please do and let the competition continue!

CHAPTER 25

Plough Back that Profit

Ayo: How are you doing today?

Tolu: I am good, but not that good.

Ayo: It is obvious; I hope it is not business-related this time.

Tolu: What else could it be if not for my business? Money matter is the real matter.

Ayo: *(Smiles)*So, you like money like this? Well, who doesn't like money? What could be the cause this time?

Tolu: The side business I am partnering with Tayo is giving me a headache.

Ayo: Really? I never knew you and Tayo were into any partnership.

Tolu: Not really a partnership like that; the thing is, they have plenty of vegetable farmers in their area since it was formerly a farm settlement, so he started buying vegetables from the farmers to sell to the market women close to the school, so I decided on giving him ₦500 to help me buy and he also graciously helps me to supply to the sellers because the demand is very high.

Ayo: So, you guys are doing cool business like that, and you never told me?

Tolu: Sorry about that; when the business needs more capital, I am sure we will involve you.

Ayo: That's not a problem, just a joke, so what really happened?

Tolu: Well, Tayo has been really helpful; by the time I give him the ₦500, he gives me ₦700, I give him ₦500 back for the business, ₦100 as his contribution and ₦100 for personal use.

Ayo: If I got you right, you return ₦500, which has always been the initial capital.

Tolu: Yes

Ayo: If I may ask, how long have you been doing this?

Tolu: This is the 3rd month, which is why it is giving me concern; it seems the business is not growing, just static.

Ayo: Hmmm! I think the fault is with you.

Tolu: How do you mean?

Ayo: After the sales, you give him ₦500 like you have always been giving. You see, Albert Einstein once said something: *"Doing the same thing the way you have always been doing it and expecting different results is the beginning of insanity"*. How would you keep giving him the same amount and expect growth or something different? You see, in business, when he gives you the ₦700, you should have given him ₦600 back as your new capital. Next time, he might make total sales of ₦900; from the ₦900, you can return ₦700 and give him ₦100, then you start taking ₦100 for personal use.

Tolu: Hmm!

Ayo: This is called plough back or return profit. Your business cannot grow beyond the capital base. You are to always add part of your profit to the capital base to grow and expand your business. This is why many entrepreneurs don't pay themselves a salary in the first few months or years of starting their business; they must keep increasing their capital base.

Tolu: You are very right.

CHAPTER 26

Partnership

Ayo: Tolu, my guy, how are you today?

Tolu: I am doing very well. In fact, I am in very high spirits.

Ayo: Wow! Load us with the gist.

Tolu: Thank you for your advice on ploughing back the profits. You see, the business is paying off now, and Tayo has been wonderful. We want to expand the business now and be supplying vegetables in larger quantities.

Tayo: That is true. We may need more people to join us now. It is becoming overwhelming for the two of us.

Bola: I can hear money calling my name. Here I am, send me!

Tayo: (*Laughing*) Bola! You love money.

James: Me too. I cannot be left out in this important discussion that promises to change my life.

Bola: Alright, come let us reason this issue together. You know they say two good heads are better than one. We have five good heads here now.

James: On a serious note, we all know that there is power in unity and agreement. Most organizations succeed when there is team spirit and teamwork, for a house divided against itself can never stand. My brother once explained one principle to me, it is called synergy, which states that 2+2=5, the result of combined actions, is greater than the sum of what individual components could have achieved separately. This means if I work on my own and you work on your own, what both of us will achieve if our individual efforts are added together will be less than if the two of us work as a team.

Bola: That is quite beautiful. No wonder the Holy writings say, "One will chase a thousand, and two will put ten thousand to flight".

Ayo: Guys, you are right; one thing comes to mind: the five of us should brainstorm and come up with ideas on how to make this business get to more people, how to make greater profits, what role each person will have to play, the capital needed, resource sharing formula and some other crucial topics.

James: That is a brilliant suggestion. Ayo, your brain is working.

Bola: Wait... But how are we going to share the profit?

Ayo: Ah! I can see why Tayo said you love money earlier on.

Bola: Of course? What is the essence of business if not to make money?

Tolu: Wait first. Let us address the important matters that Ayo raised.

James: True! However, we will still need to deliberate how we are to share the profits and losses.

Bola: I am enjoying this conversation; I know James is good at relating with people, Tolu at strategising and coming up with creative ideas, Tayo is very good with bargaining, Ayo's strength is Accounting and Bookkeeping while I am good at selling and marketing things to people. We are surely going to make a good team.

James: When it comes to handling the money, I can help out ...

Bola: I thought you said I love money.

Ayo: (*Smiles*) We all like money; since there will be proper accountability and documentation, anybody can do that.

James: I think we need to start our planning and strategising now.

CHAPTER 27

Investment

Luke: I have been looking for you since.

John: I went to the market so I could restock my shop. I hope all is well?

Luke: Yes, all is well; I just want to pass on vital information to you that can change your future financially. It is a form of venture in which you can invest your money, and it will yield returns to you over time. If you want to earn more, you need to invest more.

John: You can be funny. Is it jackpot or lotto or Betnaija or MMM? My friend, this legitimate business of mine is yielding profit, so I am good.

Luke: Well, it is a form of investment, not a Ponzi scheme like MMM, and it is not a game of luck like Nairabet.

John: So, what kind of investment are we talking about?

Luke: Well, my uncle, who works in a bank, came in yesterday to inform my dad about it. I was exposed to what investment is and how one can invest his money wisely. The three main areas he talked about were multilevel network marketing, FOREX trading and investment in shares, stocks and bonds.

John: You are still talking in parables. Can you please shed light on those areas you have mentioned? Even though I don't think I have a big amount for investment.

Luke: Network marketing is trending nowadays even though it is taking different shapes; some businesses now engage in multilevel marketing where you register and invite other people to join; as you invite other people, your level will grow, and you stand to enjoy many things depending on the company. Another form of investment is foreign exchange (FOREX), but the one I want to talk about is the buying of shares.

John: Okay. Now, I am a bit interested. How is it done?

Luke: A share is a unit of ownership that represents an equal proportion of a company's capital. This means that if you have a share in a company, you are part of the owners; you are a shareholder and entitled to part of the profits that would be shared as dividends at the end of the financial year. You can buy as many shares as you desire.

John: Wait, I heard an advertisement on the radio of a bank offering shares to the public, but I never paid attention to it because I didn't understand it.

Luke: Yes, that is it; as of this morning, it was ₦250 per share, which means you can buy as many as you like. When my dad heard about it, he gave my uncle ₦5000 to buy shares in my name.

John: You're now a 'big boy'. So, if I buy shares with part of the profit I am making, it means I will now have multiple streams of income without one affecting the other. But how do I go about it?

Luke: Yes. I will help you tell my uncle about it whenever you are ready. You can always meet an accountant, banker, stock broker, or financial analyst to assist you on how to go about it.

John: It is good to be informed that there are many areas in which one can invest his money, and it will yield interest. Imagine leaving such money for five years, how much it would have turned over.

Luke: You can say that again, instead of squandering money up and down, one can actually invest to secure one's financial future.

John: Do you know one of the greatest investments you can make as an entrepreneur is in people?

Luke: How do you mean?

John: No entrepreneur or a leader can single-handedly grow an organization or build a great empire. An entrepreneur should be able to discover potentials in people, invest in them and help them develop these potentials. An entrepreneur invests in people, and the people help him to build his business empire.

Luke: Hmm, that's deep.

CHAPTER 28

Multiple Streams of Income/Diversification

Femi: Good evening, my friend; we didn't see you at the tutorial this morning. What happened?

Chisom: I went to Lagos Island to buy new stock for my business.

Femi: Really? How did it go?

Chisom: Thanks. It went well. However, I had to spend all my money to restock. And I still need to buy that handout.

Femi: Ah! My friend, my friend. You will buy it when you start selling those stocks.

Chisom: We both know that the lecturer gave us a deadline, and if I don't meet up, I won't be allowed to write his test.

(Chidi joins their conversation)

Chidi: How are you guys doing?

Chisom: Big bro of Africa! Please, I need you to loan me five-thousand-naira ASAP so that I can buy one very important handout.

Chidi: I thought you were also doing business. Why borrow?

Chisom: Haba! Bro, aren't you aware that I just returned from the market? I spent every dime in my account.

Chidi: Ah! Do you know that friend of mine, Kosini? I also just invested a huge amount in her lucrative business idea.

Chisom: Why would you do that? Is your own business not yielding a good profit for you?

Chidi: One road doesn't lead to the market; one needs to have multiple streams of income. See, I felt comfortable diversifying by investing in her business because I am making enough profit from my own business.

Chisom: I am making profits, too; I only plunge the profit back to expand my capital base.

Chidi: That is also good. But do you know that every business has its seasons, both peak and off seasons? You can keep the profits rolling in by diversifying and having different streams of income.

Femi: I have heard another new thing today. Bros, Bros, the business tycoon. This is BIZ SENSE 401, Chisom bring jotter and pen for me.

Chisom: I am really interested in diversifying and having another source of income. But I hope you haven't forgotten the five thousand naira I talked about.

Chidi: *Haba*! Last born, I have already done the transfer, but let me show you one clean way you can diversify. See that friend of mine, Kosini that I talked about, she has very great business ideas. She even wants to start branding her goods, and she is in dire need of investors. Chisom, you can invest in that.

Chisom and Femi: Thank you.

Chidi: Don't mention. But come to think of it, Chisom, you can both equally leverage your popularity and connection on campus to also start a side business of designing and branding handouts, departmental almanacs, yearbooks, posters and the rest since Femi is a very good graphic designer and you have great business acumen.

Femi: Yes. Finally, I can convert my passion to cool cash.

CHAPTER 29

Discount

Kola: Guys, please, I want to ask a question.

Idowu and Bola: Okay, we are all ears.

Kola: Don't be offended, my friends, but do you have an idea why people keep patronizing the shopping mall down the road even though they are not the only shop selling such?

Idowu: (*Smiles*) Look at you, you are supposed to know, is it not obvious?

Bola: What is obvious, if I may ask?

Idowu: You mean you have not heard that they did use some fetish means, which makes the crowd always patronize them on a daily basis? You guys should just wake up.

Bola: Ah! Idowu! Too much of *Africa Magic Channel* is affecting your thinking; anything that is working is now a result of diabolic effects, right? Kola don't mind her.

Idowu: This is not African Magic; it is what I heard people say.

Bola: You had better be cautious of what you say before it implicates you. I am sure you guys have bought things there before. That is where we always buy our groceries. I can tell you few things that make people to always patronize them.

Idowu: Okay, I am all ears.

Bola: You see, apart from the fact that you will see anything you need in the shop, which reduces the stress and time of going to the main market, they have customer-friendly staff that attend to you promptly. They sell good quality products, and above all, they give discounts on their products.

Kola: Discount? What do you mean by that?

Bola: Well, the discount is the reduction in the price of goods or services as a result of prompt payment or bulk purchase.

Kola: Which means that if you buy something in bulk, or if you pay at the expected time, they will reduce the amount you are to pay?

Bola: Exactly! You know everybody likes free things and we always look for where we can get quality products at reasonable and affordable price, so rather than travel miles down to the main market, people prefer to buy from the mall.

Idowu: Ah! It is not good to spread information one is not sure about; I only overheard some women saying it the other time, and I concluded they were right. I think that news is just to blackmail the mall.

Kola: Well, some people will always cook up negative news to bring others down. Idowu, now I understand. Imagine I sell three pieces of sweets at ₦10 and Bola sells the same sweet at ₦10 per one; who will you buy from? Or if I remove 5% from the cost of what you buy but Bola doesn't, from whom will you buy your things?

Idowu: You, of course.

Kola: That is exactly what the mall does. Discounts are given to increase sales by luring both old and new customers to patronize you. One needs to embrace discounts and promos from time to time.

Idowu: No wonder I always see 5% discounts on the banner in front of Mr. Biggs on every plate of food purchased.

Bola: Discounts have a way of encouraging bulk purchases and prompt payment. Trade discount is given on bulk purchase wile cash discount is on prompt payment.

Idowu: I see, so when I buy something in bulk, they give me a trade discount, and when I pay promptly, I am given a cash discount.

Kola: Exactly!

Idowu: Thank you so much; that's a big lesson on how to increase patronage from people in business.

CHAPTER 30

Courtesy and Gratitude

Joan: Titi, there was a statement I heard Mum tell a seller yesterday that I would like you to explain to me.

Titi: What could that be?

Joan: Mum told the seller that Customers are the kings.

Titi: (*Smiles*) I have heard it many times; some will even say customers are always right. I believe it means that customers are to be treated with respect and accorded honour just like you do a king. You don't treat your customers with contempt; besides, there is no business without customers. Will you consume your goods alone?

Joan: I see. So, people go into business because of potential customers.

Titi: Yes, of course. If they fail to patronize you, you will stop being in business; you are in business because of them. So, you must always treat them well; when they come, you greet them, and even if they look younger than you, you show courtesy and respect.

Joan: Being a seller in your business is like telecommunications companies' customer service.

Titi: Exactly! When you call customer service, you see the way they answer you; they show much courtesy and receive you warmly because if you fail to patronize them, they will be affected, and just one customer can spoil their sales (market). Even after they patronize you, you are to show gratitude and appreciation, which will keep them coming.

Joan: That is true; treating customers well can also make them recommend others to patronize you.

Titi: That is another powerful point you just made. You see, beyond the adverts you place on media houses, customers' opinions about you go a long way. I know many students who came to this school because of my mum's testimony about the quality of teachers we have here. So, when you treat customers well, they will help you market and advertise your business by speaking well about you to people, but when you treat them badly, they also speak negatively about you.

Joan: Wow! I totally agree with you, but what about some customers who are just there to foment troubles like the devil? How do you treat such?

Titi: Hmmm! It's not always easy to treat some customers well; that is why wisdom and patience are required. A hot-tempered person cannot be in business because some customers haggle the prices of goods irrationally. Some can be very provoking, but in all, one must maintain calmness.

Joan: Seriously, it generally takes patience and wisdom to deal with people. How much more, business matters that involve money.

Titi: You like money and diamonds, right? Visualize your customers as bags filled with money. You know, like boxes filled with diamonds. Treat them the way you will treat your money sacks or diamond boxes. I am sure you won't want to lose your money bag or diamond box.

Joan: Never! I will guard it jealously and treat it with special care. I will even check on it every now and then to ensure it is still intact.

Titi: Good. In all, we should try our best to receive them well whenever they come; good reception creates good impressions. It appeals to their emotions to buy from us and remember that the first impression lasts longer.

Joan: That is the secret to winning potential customers to your side and further keeping them.

Titi: You can say that again, but it must be backed with integrity.

Joan: Can you shed light on that, please?

Titi: I will do that after the class; they have rung the bell for the next class.

Titi: I will do that after the class; they have rung the bell for the next class.

CHAPTER 31

Integrity

Joan: My special business consultant.

Titi: (*Smiles*). Very soon, you guys will start paying consultation fee.

Joan: No problem, but where do you get all these business tips and ideas?

Titi: (*Smiles*) Well, I learn from my mum and my elder sister. Once in a while, I listen to the news, study the biographies of successful entrepreneurs, read business books, study people doing business in my neighbourhood, and ask our business studies teacher questions.

Joan: No wonder you are mostly with him during break-time. But how do you have time for all these yet not lagging behind in your academics?

Titi: (*Smiles*) Well, it is all about proper planning and setting my priorities right. I know where I am going and what it entails to get there, so I am always motivated to strive more. It has not been easy because I have to sacrifice many things. I believe in my vision, and I know where I am going. That's what keeps me going.

Joan: I must submit to you that you are such a bundle of talent and a blessing to me.

Titi: Thanks, friend. So, regarding the question you asked the other time about how integrity can help promote business, integrity is the quality of being honest and fair. The love for quick money has made many businessmen compromise their stand for quality and excellence. Some have lied about the prices of goods, and some have sold fake products as original, which have killed some innocent persons. Some have defrauded others, while some have sold expired, substandard, contraband products all because of greed, covetousness and lack of integrity.

Joan: I can relate to that; my uncle once stopped me from buying drugs at the Chemist down our street because he once bought a fake drug there; my uncle's wife almost died because of the drug the Chemist administered to her.

Titi: Can you see what I am saying now? People sell fake drugs, use chemicals that have been banned from circulation, and adjust their measurement scales; some will even mix good products with bad and many other evil acts people do in business today. I heard the story of a woman who had a crèche. The girl employed to take care of the children mistakenly breastfed another baby with another woman's expressed breast milk. When the owner got to know, she was advised to cover it up, but she instead invited the two parents; this led to serious charges, and many tests were carried out to make sure the baby was not infected. Although the woman wanted to press further charges for negligence, she later changed her mind after considering the fact that the owner could have easily covered it up but didn't. She realized it was her integrity that made her open up. This made her to withdraw the charges. Not only that, she recommended the crèche to her friends in need of crèche with integrity.

Joan: Imagine! It is not easy to maintain integrity with the way people want to become rich at the expense of others.

Titi: That is the evil in our world today, but we have to stand up for what is right when doing business. It pays to have integrity in business. Even though it may be challenging at the start, it pays at the end. Nothing good can stand on the legs of falsehood; it is a matter of time; the weight of that good thing will paralyze the legs of falsehood because falsehood doesn't have the strength to carry the weight of good things. It is a matter of time before people who lack integrity are forced out of business. Only those with integrity will stand.

Joan: Seriously, the way people lie in business these days is disturbing.

Titi: But it pays to have integrity in doing business and in whatever we do. I have heard the story of a man who gave goods to a supplier to pay later without paying a dime because he had integrity. Integrity helps people to believe you, take you by your words, vouch for you, and recommend people to you. In summary, we should be truthful with our words, act in the sincerity of our heart and do to others what we would like them to do to us, for what goes around comes around.

CHAPTER 32

Customer Service/Public Relations

Titi: Joan! This one, you are sweating like this; where are you coming from with this bag in your hand?

Joan: Good afternoon, Titi. I went to buy beverages for Mum at the shop down the road.

Titi: Ah! Why that distance? But Madam Lala Stores is just next block to yours, and the last time I checked, she sells beverages, too. Or is it that her prices are too high or that she sells fake stuff?

Joan: Well, neither of the two. The main reason why we stopped buying from her is because of her poor reception of customers. We used to buy things from her before, but just like many other people, we only tolerated her approach to customers, hoping she would change. Can you imagine what happened just this morning when I was passing her shop, she and a customer were busy trading words, curses and abuses at each other like girls fighting over a boyfriend.

Titi: You cracked me there. Give me the full gist while we walk home together.

Joan: Don't mind her; the customer asked her how much she sold her tin of milk, and she said ₦180. The customer then asked if she could take it for ₦150, and that was it. What didn't she say to insult the woman? "Come and take it, thief, *barawo banza*! As if I bought it for that price, you want to run my business down like that of your father, it won't work…"

Titi: Are you kidding me? You mean she went that far?

Joan: Hmmm... She said more than that; it took the intervention of passersby to salvage the situation.

Titi: That is serious. If that is the case, I will never go to her shop to buy anything *before someone will come and insult my ancestors on top of my own money.*

Joan: I am telling you. I don't even know which is more annoying; you will have to greet her several times before her royal majesty will answer you like she is doing you a favour or the fact that she will be singing songs to insult you when you pass without greeting her.

Titi: In marketing, is it not the seller that is supposed to greet the potential customer first? More so, the seller must do so cheerfully too.

Joan: Of course, that is the way it was supposed to be. Anyways, that is her cup of tea. It is a lesson to us, too, that whenever we venture into business, we must have good customer care and public relations.

CHAPTER 33

Complimenting People and Business

Titi: You look so beautiful this morning, as always; I like the fragrance you're wearing.

Joan: I am blushing; you are flattering me.

Titi: How will I do such? I am only appreciating the work of God in your life.

Joan: Thanks for the compliments; you are actually a darling. You make me feel appreciated and wanted, and you make me feel good about myself.

Titi: You are welcome. Actually, it is always good to compliment and appreciate people. It can open you to the worlds of ideas in business and connections.

Joan: How do you mean?

Titi: It makes people feel free around you. You remember there is a saying that your dressing is not complete until you wear a smile. When you smile at people and compliment them, they are able to relate freely with you. Smiles have a way of softening the hearts of people. Let me share a story with you of how my sister got her first international connection. One day, she met a lady in her hostel, and she complimented her on her perfume. That made the following conversation ensued between them.

(Conversation between Titi's sister, Loveth and Rose, a new student on Campus)

Rose: Good day, Senior. Please, ma'am, where can I get a business centre to make photocopies?

Loveth: (*Smiling*)Hello, sis. I guess you are a new student.

Rose: Yes, ma, I am a fresher.

Loveth: You are welcome to Campus life. There is one behind this block.

Rose: Thank you very much, ma.

Loveth: (*Laughs cheerfully*) *Please, oh! Which one is ma and which one is senior again oh?* This is not a Secondary school. I am Loveth, by the way. You?

Rose: My name is Rose m... Ah! sorry (*chuckles*)

Loveth: I like this fragrance of yours

Rose: (*Smiles*) Thank you.

Loveth: Can I please know the name? The fragrance is not that common.

Rose: Well, I actually brought it from the United States.

Loveth: No wonder, how I wish I can get it here in the country. They must be quite expensive though.

Rose: Well, they are not that expensive; only the exchange rate might affect the price.

Loveth: Like, how much are they over there?

Rose: Like $2 but with the current exchange rate in the country, maybe ₦2800. Aside shipping cost and other arrangements.

Loveth: I am thinking of selling it here to the ladies on Campus since they like imported stuff, and this is not common. I know many of them will want to buy it.

Rose: That is a cool idea, I can actually tell my aunt over there to help get some down when bringing in some of her goods, with that, the cost will reduce.

Loveth: That will be lovely. Let me have your contact information so we can discuss how to go about it.

Rose: (*Smiles*) Okay. Nice to meet you today.

(*Conversation ends*)

Joan: Oh wow! Can I say again that you are a blessing to me?

Titi: (*Chuckles*) Yes, you can, since it is me you are now using for practical.

(*Joan & Titi both laugh cheerfully*)

CHAPTER 34

Enthusiasm

Loveth: It is good to have '*oyaya*' in business.

Rose: '*Oyaya*'! What is *oyaya*?

Loveth: Oh! The English word just escaped my mind, but let me explain it.

Rose: Okay, explain it; let me see if I have heard it before.

Loveth: When a seller is all out to persuade and convince a buyer to buy what she is selling by her warm reception, sweet words, and captivating smiles, I mean when the seller tries to make you see reasons why you should buy from her even when you try to pass her shop.

Rose: Where did you hear the word?

Loveth: I followed Mum to the market on Saturday; when we got there, we bought other things remaining garri. We passed the first garri seller, but she just sat down on a chair playing with her phone; mum didn't stop there and moved to the second woman. Mum asked for the price of her garri; Mum tried to haggle the price, but she declined harshly, so we left her. As soon as we left that shop, we saw another woman beckoning at us with an inviting smile; when we almost got to her, she started with her sweet words, please buy my garri, it is '*garri Egba*', it is very crunchy, it is good for making '*eba*', and it is good for drinking. Mum asked for the price, and she said ₦150 per module; Mum said ₦130; she started begging Mum to please pay ₦140 because she, too, bought it at ₦130. The way she attended to us was so warm; her smile already appealed to me, and I wanted Mum to buy from her.

Rose: *Did you now finally buy from her?*

Loveth: Yes, of course. I felt so happy. I told Mum I wanted her to buy from her because of her warm reception. Mum said she has *oyaya*, and every businesswoman must also have it; even if the customer wants to go, you still try to persuade her to buy from you, you don't just give up on a customer.

Rose: I think I now have an idea of what *oyaya* is; it is enthusiasm. Yoruba people call it *oro aje*, which can be said to be an effort we make to promote our business. Enthusiasm is a strong excitement about something, a strong feeling of active interest in something that you really like or enjoy. It is the inner joy, happiness, excitement, and drive that reflects in the way you treat people or do your business.

Loveth: *Ah! So, Yankee babe like you understand Yoruba like this.*

Rose: (*Laughs*). My mum speaks Yoruba to me, and I watch a lot of Yoruba movies.

Loveth: *You see, I started applying oyaya and oro aje to this my perfume business at home, and I sold over 12 pieces.*

Rose: Senior Loveth, you are on point, ma.

Loveth: Of course, junior Rose.

CHAPTER 35

Diligence

Loveth: Salma! Salma! Wake up! Didn't you say you have a class by 9 am?

Rose: You better wake up. It is 8:30 am!

Salma: Oh God! Loveth, why will you and your friend not allow someone to enjoy her sleep in this room?

Rose: Salma, the way you sleep in this room, are you preparing for a sleeping competition?

Tonto: *Don't mind her she doesn't know more than sleep.* She can sleep from morning till night. I wonder how she does it; she sleeps all day yet still sleeps at night. I guess sleep is her hobby. I am sure she sleeps in class too.

Rose: You have forgotten the proverbs that say, "A little sleep, a little slumber, a little folding of the hands to sleep and poverty will overtake you like a bandit."

Tonto: Oh! Tell her.

Loveth: Enough, you two! *You Tonto talking about someone that sleeps a lot, are you not the laziest person in this room?* When it comes to work, you have a way of running away from it; you don't wash plates, nor do you sweep the room or cook your food. Have you forgotten that God doesn't bless laziness, and He doesn't reward idleness? Have you forgotten the part of the Bible that says, *'See thou a man diligent in his business, He will stand before kings and not mean men?'* It is the works of our hands that God will bless.

Salma: Tell her she likes correcting others without correcting herself.

Loveth: You too, keep quiet. What is the difference between the two of you? We agree that you are hardworking and don't run away from work like her, but you, too, have to be forced before you know you will work. Most times, you will just do it halfway or do it late. One thing I would like you all to know is that to be successful in life, you must be hardworking, diligent, and engage in all you do with the whole of your heart. Remember the proverb that says, "Whatsoever your hands find to do, do it with all of your might." This is the secret of my business: if I had been lazy, I wouldn't be where I am today. I am sure if Dangote slept like you, he wouldn't be where he is today. Many of you sing 2face and Olamide's songs, but haven't you heard them say they work most of the time all night trying to mix and produce their songs in the studio? You see, to be successful in life, you can't afford to be lazy or sleep your life away. Building a great empire is not by wishful thinking but by working hard and working smart.

Rose: You see why I call you Senior Loveth. You are so full of wisdom.

Tonto: Loveth, we didn't realize these attitudes will affect us in the near future.

Salma: Let me quickly take my bath, so I won't miss my class.

CHAPTER 36

Humility

Titi: Joan, I was just coming from your house and was told you went to the market.

Joan: Yes. You know that as the only girl in the house, I have automatically become the only candidate for market runs. *But this one, you are looking for me like this. Is there anything good for your girl?*

Titi: *Yes, there is one vital secret I have just discovered on how to grow this our new business.*

Joan: (*Smiles*) That's my beautiful business partner. You will not cease to amaze me with your business acumen and passion for business. Should we discuss it here or go inside?

Titi: No time to waste. I will soon go back home to attend to my assignments. Did you listen to Fresh FM today?

Joan: Nay, I just got back from the market, like I told you.

Titi: Can you believe the radio station has now been crowned the best radio station for the year 2018/2019? In just four years of its existence. When there are other radio stations with many years of experience, interestingly, this would be the first time a radio station in Ibadan would be nominated for the award, let alone get it.

Joan: I am so happy for them. I know they have some fascinating programmes that I like to listen to but I am yet to get the principle of growing business you want to talk about.

Titi: I know that is where your mind is. But what do you think the secret could be?

Joan: Maybe their innovative programmes, the parade of wonderful presenters and OAPs, their wide coverage because they have lots of foreign listeners that even call into their programmes and probably out of the sympathy they got from the masses after the former governor demolished their station which got national and international reactions.

Titi: Well, all the points could have also played out, but I know some radio stations that have wonderful OAPs with wide coverage and beautiful programmes, but one thing I believed really helped them to be crowned the best radio station aside the God factor is the attitude of the Owner, Dr. Yinka Ayefele to his staff, audience and people at large. The man is so humble, friendly and cheerful. See the way he interacts and relates with his staff as if they are his family members; you will barely know he employed them and paid their salaries. How do you expect his workers not to be loyal to him?

Joan: Wow! I like your insightful thought. I totally agree with you. There is this show he anchors with EOB; even though he employed him, the two of them crack jokes, tease and make jest of each other as if they are fellow workers.

Titi: You got my point exactly. Despite his popularity, wealth and connection as a musician, he is still down-to-earth, accessible and approachable.

Joan: You remember one of his concerts that we attended? One of his workers even made a joke to tease him; he just laughed over it.

Titi: Yes, he doesn't just relate well with his workers; he also relates well with his fans and listeners; this has expanded his level of influence in society and endeared him to the hearts of the people. I believe this was part of why he was able to attract the masses that rallied around him when the former governor demolished the station.

Joan: Yes, someone once said the last time he saw a crowd gather like that in their numbers in solidarity was when MKO died. He had been able to win the hearts of his listeners with his humility and simplicity.

Titi: I believe it pays to be humble in business, no matter the height one attains, treat your workers/staff well, treat your business partners well, and treat your customers well. I believe because he treats his staff well, they are loyal to him and give their best, which translates to the satisfaction the online viewers/listeners enjoy. The rippling effect of that is what made the station win the best radio station for the year. You see, some CEOs look down on their staff and treat them like they can never amount to anything in life. They act like 'God' to both workers and customers, and they don't give a damn when a customer complains; they'd rather tell such to go to hell.

Joan: I can relate to that; Mum resigned from her former place of work because of the arrogant behaviour of her former boss. Mum had to start her own, just like you know. The woman would bash workers, abuse them, treat them like slaves, and at times, she paid salaries late without an apology; how does she expect the people to be happy and excited working for her? When your workers don't work with joy, you can't get the best out of them. So it is always good to make your workers happy, and one of the ways you do that is to relate with them well and treat them as humans, not as slaves.

Titi: You have said it all. Though one should be firm, humility is very keen to grow your business.

Joan: We are surely getting there too; I will put this secret in my left hand so as not to eat with it and lose it.

CHAPTER 37

Honesty in Business

Joan: TJ, I have been looking at you from afar, laughing like somebody who won a jackpot.

TJ: (*Laughs*) You see, I didn't just win a jackpot; it is a luck pot. You can't believe what just happened. I just sold ten cartons of noodles at the rate of ₦4,000 per one. I made a profit of more than ₦10,000.

Titi: Wow! How come? How did you do it? Market price of noodles is ₦3,100 so where did the excessive profit come from?

TJ: Well, you know how it's done in business.

Titi: Please enlighten us.

TJ: Well, those were old stock; I bought the stock when the price was as low as ₦2,500 per carton. Do you know the items will soon expire? I was able to clean part of the expiration date of the cartons. The man told me he was going to donate them to an orphanage home so he wouldn't even notice.

Joan: Oh my God! TJ, don't you realize you were dubious? Not only that, but you were also completely dishonest!

TJ: *You are the one seeing it as that, oh.* It is part of business strategies; besides, anyone in business should know how to lie.

Titi: Hmm... I am still in shock. Have you forgotten they say honesty is the best policy?

TJ: That was then; you have to be wise in our era. Even the government lie; some pastors lie to collect money from their members, so we are all in the lying business. It is not only lawyers that are liars, all are liars.

Joan: This is becoming unbecoming! Once, you lied to a customer that the goods were imported, yet they were local goods packed in imported packs. The last time, you also sold fake products as the original products, and you collected the price for the original ones. Choi!

TJ: Are you trying to judge me? Everybody is doing it; all those people you see driving big cars, opening other business outlets, diversifying and growing their business, how do you think they do it? You need to wake up from your sleep.

Joan: I am not your judge. Have you considered that what goes around comes around? Let him who lives in a glass house not throw stones.

TJ: I think you need to start going now; you are beginning to get on my nerves. Who are you to tell me how to run my business?

Titi: Well, I will go. Don't say I didn't warn you.

(A few months later, TJ's daughter went to her dad's shop in her dad's absence and drank a sachet of Caprisonne, unknown to her that it was fake. She almost died from food poisoning)

TJ: (*Referring to Joan and Titi*) My sisters, I am sorry for the way I spoke rudely to you the last time. I didn't know my evil deeds would catch up with me like that. I nearly lost my daughter.

Joan: Thank God you learnt your lesson, but everyone now knows about your shady business, and they have now stopped patronizing you. So, in all of these, what did you gain?

TJ: Hmmm... I have really learnt my lessons; I have to start over and I must build my integrity from the scratch by being honest.

Joan: Better!

CHAPTER 38

Excellence

Rose: Loveth, let us go and buy *Akara* at Mama Fatima's shop.

Loveth: Will she be there by now? I think she opens at 5 p.m.

Rose: I saw her on my way from class.

Loveth: Okay, let us go there.

Rose: Good evening, ma. Please, we want to buy *Akara*.

Mama Fatima: How much *Akara* do you want to buy?

Loveth: Give me ₦100 own.

Mama Fatima: What about you, my daughter?

Rose: Don't worry, ma, I am not buying.

Loveth: Come, what stunt did you just pull there? You asked us to come here to buy *Akara,* but you didn't buy?

Rose: I am so sorry, friend; I know I initiated the move to come here to buy bean cake, but the way she packed your own disgusts me. I don't know why people are so carefree in business. Buying things in this country can be discouraging; I see mediocrity everywhere. You see, one of the things common among United States businessmen is excellence. Excellence is manifested in the way they manufacture their products, the way they package them and the way they even sell them.

Loveth: Please! Don't bring your Yankee mentality here. You have been in *Naija* long enough to know this is the norm. You know most of the people selling here are uneducated and petty traders.

Rose: That is not an excuse; you don't have to go to school to embrace excellence, you don't need to be a big trader to embrace excellence. Excellence is who you are; it is the spirit at work in a man. Excellence is a function of your nature, perception, belief system, and mindset. A man with an excellent spirit will always strive to be the best and offer the best in all he does. Excellence makes you choose quality in all you do.

Loveth: Whenever you enter this mode, I get amused.

Rose: See examples before our own eyes. See Ekaette, who sells food. Is she educated? See how neat her shop is and how she packages her food. Mama Kemi, who sells fried yam and potatoes, is she educated? But isn't her packaging amazing? Please, I will buy my *Akara* from Halima; though she doesn't even understand English, she is neat, always smiles, and her funny way of painting her face in the name of make-up implies she is making an effort to be excellent in what she does.

Loveth: Okay, oh! Buy, and let's go back.

CHAPTER 39

Trade

Collins: It seems everyone is involved in one business or the other to survive on Campus; let's start a trade, too.

Andy: You said? Stop being funny. You don't look like someone who has a passion for trading to me.

Collins: Really? *Haba!* Andy, is it written on someone's forehead? I want to make money in this life. Don't you want to make money in life?

Andy: What kind of question is that? Who doesn't want to make money?

Collins: The question is, what is money? Is money not a medium of exchange for payment of goods and services? So, if you want money, you must be able to give something of value that somebody will be willing and ready to pay for, and that is what Trade is about.

Andy: (*Smiles*) We are all traders in life; every one that is successful in life is a trader, but it's like you only see traders as people who buy and sell goods.

Collins: Yes, of course.

Andy: Well, my understanding of trading goes beyond that. Trade simply means to exchange. It is the activity or process of buying, selling or exchanging goods or services, and it can also be the exchange of value for money while a trader is a person who engages in an occupation, business or industry.

Collins: Hmmm, so trading goes beyond buying and selling goods.

Andy: Yes, trade is just a form of exchange; you give what you have to receive what you need; it can be tangible or intangible.

It can be an idea, knowledge, talent, skill, or information that you are ready to give out for people to buy.

Collins: That means doctors, engineers, teachers, and professors are traders, too?

Andy: Yes, everybody is a trader, and we are all expected to trade what we have for what we need. We are just to make sure we package what we have in a way that appeals to and adds value to consumers. So, what do you intend to trade?

Collins: You really caught me off guard with your knowledge. Seriously, I haven't given much thought to what I can trade in exchange for money. All I know is that I have some savings and I am good at marketing things. I will definitely ponder on this more deeply.

Andy: That is beautiful. Just remember: not everybody will have what you need, and not everybody will need what you have. Do you remember the barter system before the advent of money? You look for who has what you need and needs what you have. If you have yam but need beans, you will look for who has beans and needs yam. The more you can connect with those who need what you have, the more you will be able to meet your own needs. So, if you want to make more money, get more people to pay for what you have. The earlier you discover what you can trade in, the better for you. It must always be a win-win situation. As for me, I would rather trade with my skills.

Collins: I am sure it is your business consultation skills you are referring to here. Thanks, bro. This is my stop. See you later.

CHAPTER 40

Carry out Feasibility Studies

Uncle John: Taiwo Taiwo, how are you doing? I believe you're doing fine with your studies.

Taiwo: Fine, sir, and yes, all is going on well.

Uncle John: Good to hear.

Taiwo: Yes, uncle.

Uncle John: Let me advise you. You are not too young to start planning for your future. You can see the situation in the country; don't just think everything is about going to school and getting certificates. When we were your age, by the time a young man/lady graduates from university, a good job with lots of benefits awaits such graduates, but there are no jobs out there now. This week alone, I have received more than 20 CVs from people who want my assistance in securing a job for them, a job I haven't seen. I always advise my children and those close to me that it is not too early to acquire a vocational skill or business sense. Thank God for you. Your mum is a businesswoman, and you can always learn from her.

Taiwo: Uncle, you are in the spirit. I even came here because I have a business idea, I want to discuss with you to see if you can help me finance it.

Uncle John: Wow! That's beautiful. You are beginning to reason like an adult and take responsibility for your life and future, unlike your twin, Kenny. I am impressed.

Taiwo: (*Laughs*)Yes! That is true, sir; I don't want to be like Bro Tunji, who has been looking for a collar job for more than three years after his NYSC programme. It was his parents who pressured him to pick up a teaching job rather than staying idle at home.

Uncle John: Who is Tunji?

Taiwo: He is our neighbour's son, and he assists me with my school lessons once in a while.

Uncle John: It is better than doing nothing; everybody is busy hustling up and down. I hope God delivers us one day in this country, though it is everywhere.

Taiwo: Amen! But he has already stopped the teaching job because of the meagre salary he was paid. This has caused lots of disagreement between him and his parents, who see him as a lazy person.

Uncle John: Maybe he should get a skill.

Taiwo: Uncle, to avoid what happened to Uncle Tunji, it's better that I start a business now.

Uncle John: That is my Taiwo, but have you carried out the feasibilities stu...

Taiwo: Fisi...What???

Uncle John: Feasibility studies.

Taiwo: What is that one, sir?

Uncle John: It is the survey or test you carry out to know if a plan or idea will succeed or not. Before you venture into a business, you have to strategize and get the opinion of the people there in a way to know if they would need the service you intend to render or the products you intend to sell. Can such an idea fly in such an environment? Are there already existing sellers or producers of that intended product? It also involves carrying out a market survey of the place, how much it may cost you to start, how much you will sell to make a profit or break even, and how much the people would be able to afford it.

Taiwo: Thank you so much, sir; I haven't done that, sir.

Uncle John: It is very important you do that. Many businesses fold up because they never took the time to test the waters by carrying out feasibility studies; they rushed to start, only to later discover they were on the wrong track. You must be able to meet the needs of the people in ways they can afford your products. For example, you don't build a fast-food centre in areas you know the people cannot afford it. Availability and affordability are vital factors to consider when venturing into business.

Taiwo: I will surely get back to you after I have carried out the feasibility studies.

Uncle John: You are always welcome, my son. Also, ensure you prepare a business plan; it is very crucial, too. When you are through, we can talk about the financial aspect— my regards to Kenny.

Taiwo: Thank you so much, sir. She will hear.

CHAPTER 41

Business Plan

Taiwo: Hello Andy, please, do you have an idea of what a business plan is? I went to meet my uncle about my business idea. I wanted to see if he could help me out with the capital, but he asked me to carry out a feasibility study and come up with a business plan.

Andy: Have you carried out the feasibility studies?

Taiwo: Yes, but I will still need your professional input to perfect it. However, my major concern is drafting the business plan.

Andy: Well, that is very easy; you know it is always good to have a business plan before venturing into business. It is just like the builders of a house; before they start the building, they always draw the plan. A business plan is a summary of how a business owner, manager or entrepreneur intends to organize an entrepreneurial endeavour and implement activities necessary and sufficient for the venture to succeed. In summary, a business plan is a road map that provides directions for a business to achieve its goals. This helps to avoid bumps in the road.

Taiwo: What are the components of a business plan?

Andy: A business plan has the nature of the business, for example, selling foodstuff, dry cleaning and laundry business. It contains the name of the business, the address/location of the business, the objectives of the business, the budget of the business in other words, the estimated income and expenditure, the nature/type of the product or service, likely competitors, marketing strategy to advertise and make the public aware of your products, distribution channels and business management strategy.

Taiwo: I never knew there is more to business than just having an idea and the capital to finance it.

Andy: A business plan helps you to clarify your thoughts, guides you, attracts investors, and reduces risks in business.

Taiwo: Thank you so much, my friend; I hope you will assist me in drafting it.

Andy: With all pleasure. You know my consultancy fee.

Taiwo: Yes, Is it not ₦5,000? I came prepared.

Andy: I trust you. Let's get to business!

CHAPTER 42

No Pain, No Gain

Mum: Caro! Caro! Caro!

Caroline: Yes, mummy!

Mum: The *moin moin* is ready; you will now take it and sell it around the neighbourhood.

Caroline: Mum, you know I can't do that; I will become a laughing stock in the neighbourhood, and my schoolmates in the area will take the information to the school, and I will become the subject of discussions. Mum, please, I can't.

Mum: Are you out of your mind? Where do you expect me to get the money for school fees and upkeep for you and your brother? Have you seen any man helping out since your father abandoned us? How many of his family members have you seen here to help us? I still do everything possible to make you happy; you are talking about people making jest of you; who are the people? Are they the ones paying your school fees? You had better quickly go and sell them before they get cold, and labourers on the site down the road would have to buy other food.

(She reluctantly carried the cooler of moin-moin and met Ayo on the way)

Ayo: Caro, why are you frowning, and what do you have in this big cooler?

Caroline: I am tired of my family; I wonder why I was born there in the first place. I wish I had been born to Otedola's or Bill Gates's family.

Ayo: Hmmm, that's heart-touching, but why?

Caroline: Imagine mum asked me to go about hawking *moin-moin* all over the street so that I can become a laughing stock in the neighborhood.

Ayo: Caro! Caro! Caro! How many times did I call you?

Caroline: I don't know because my mind wasn't there.

Ayo: I know you are currently pissed, but I must tell you the truth, we have been friends for more than six years. Right from primary school up till now, who has been paying your school fees?

Caroline: *(Reluctantly answers)* Mum.

Ayo: Who provides food for you and Collins, your brother?

Caroline: Mum.

Ayo: Who buys your clothes and makes sure you both are comfortable?

Caroline: Mum, of course. Why all these questions?

Ayo: How much do you think she receives from her place of work? Do you think that the money is enough to cater for you all? You may not like it, and you may not be happy with the current situation; it is just a phase in life, so I want you to encourage your mum. Almost every successful businessman you see today has stories to tell. I remember hearing the story of MKO Abiola, who was once one of the richest men in Nigeria; he hawked firewood to sponsor his education. You see, your beginning might be small, but your latter end shall greatly increase. Don't be ashamed of what is gainful. You selling *moin-moin* today doesn't mean you will sell it forever. Please don't mind what people say. As much as they are not the ones paying your school fees or putting food on your table, their opinions don't matter. Besides, hawking *moin-moin* is not stealing. You know, you are a gorgeous girl; some other mothers would not mind you getting involved in a less honourable act to cater for the family. Babe, support Mum so that she doesn't develop hypertension.

Caroline: Hmm...

Ayo: I would like you to understand that helping Mum to hawk *Moin-moin* is helping yourself. It will give you the platform to build your business skills; it will build boldness and confidence in you, and it will build your interpersonal, marketing and communication skills. Just take this as an opportunity to make your future better. Remember, adversity provides excellent advantages depending on your perception. Turn your adversity to your advantage.

Caroline: Thank you so much, my friend. You have given me reasons to go on; when I get home, I will apologize to her.

Ayo: You are most welcome, my friend. *I will follow you to sell today since I don't have much work to do at home now.*

Caroline: What a friend I have found in you!

CHAPTER 43

Risk Factor

Taiwo: Collins, Collins, how are you this morning?

Collins: I am doing fine, how about you?

Taiwo: I am great, but I have an issue bothering me that has made me lose my sleep for days now.

Collins: I can see it all over your face. Hmm... What could be bothering you this much?

Taiwo: Even though I have carried out feasibility studies and drafted my business plan, launching it is of great concern to me. I get scared any time I want to launch out. What if people do not patronize me? What if the business does not grow? What if my money is lost in the business?

Collins: *(Smiles)* You see, I have told you times without numbers that everything in life is a risk, and starting a business is not left out. If you ask all successful people in any field, they will tell you they took a step of risk. Nobody knows what will happen in the next minute. Nobody can predict the future; nobody can predict the actions, reactions, perceptions and reception of people to a product accurately until it is available in the public domain. Nobody has an accurate knowledge of how people will receive their ideas or products. Every business owner speculates and hopes that people will patronize his/her product when launching it. If you try to wait for a perfect time to start, you will wait forever.

Taiwo: I entirely agree with you, but for the fear that wells up in me.

Collins: I think you need to conquer your fears by taking that risk. One of the attributes of an entrepreneur is that they are risk-takers. Before I started my business, I felt that way too, but some stories of successful people motivated me to launch out. See Andy coming; let us find out from him how you can overcome this fear.

(Both of them walk to Andy)

Collins and Taiwo: Good morning, Andy.

Andy: Good morning, my people.

Taiwo: Please, we want to find out how someone can start a business, especially when he is afraid to launch out.

Andy: This is an interesting question because every successful businessman faces such a challenge. First, you will need to encourage yourself. You need to say to yourself, "Failing wouldn't kill me; it will only allow me to know how to do it better and how not to do it." There is the story of four lepers who were cast out of a town because of their skin disease. After a while, the town started to experience drought. However, the neighbouring towns had an abundance of food, but both towns were at war with each other. The lepers thought, *"If we remain here, we will definitely die of hunger, but if we go to the camp of the enemy, two things might likely happen: either the people spare us and give us food or kill us."* In the end, they decided to take that risk and went to the neighbouring town, only to get there and discover that the enemies had fled their town, leaving their treasury, food, and all the other valuables. You see, there are always two outcomes to every step we take in life: either it turns out to be a blessing or becomes a lesson. Either way, it is still for our good. Life is all a risk, so we have to take the Bull by the horns. Remember, nothing ventured, nothing gained. The only thing is that when we are afraid, we should try to keep our minds on positive outcomes.

Taiwo: Wow! I am actually thrilled by that story of 4 lepers; it has motivated me to try my luck. After all, if it doesn't work out, I would only end up gaining experience of how not to do business. But I am sure this one will work!

Collins: That's the spirit, my brother. Thank you so much, Andy. Any time we have any other business issues, we will surely consult you for your business wisdom and counsel.

Andy: You are welcome. Next time, it won't be free.

CHAPTER 44

Calculated Risk

Collins: See the excitement all over you; what could be the secret?

Taiwo: *(Smiles)*You can say that again. I feel excited about this business. I feel I'm ready to start now.

Collins: I so much like your spirit. Many people are always scared of taking such risks, but being so happy to put your money into such a business shows how courageous and optimistic you are, which are characteristics of an entrepreneur.

Taiwo: Yes oo. Weren't you the one who said life is all about taking a risk, or have you forgotten you also said that entrepreneurs are risk-takers?

Collins: Well, I haven't forgotten, but it is always good to test the waters before jumping in. This is called a calculated risk.

Taiwo: Which one is calculated risk again? Risk is risk. If it works, fine, and if not okay, it is all a game of probability.

Collins: You are right, only that carrying out calculated risk will reduce likely losses and failures.

Taiwo: So how do I go about calculating my risk when it is not mathematics?

Collins: *(Smiles)* You see, there is nothing much, though, after you have carried out feasibility studies on your business idea. There is a need to test the reception of people to similar products in existence, test the way people will react to the advent of new products, and sample the opinions of people on what you are about to do. Don't just assume or do guesswork. Many businesses died on arrival because proper calculations were not made; they assumed people would love the business idea, not knowing the needs of the people. Don't act based on assumptions; assumption is the least important form of knowledge. Get adequate information so that you will be able to choose rightly, listen to the news, and study your environment. The more information you have, the more chances you will make the right choice and the fewer mistakes you will make. You study, observe, ask questions, and evaluate the likely outcomes objectively. Get existing samples of related products, look for their limitations and strengths, and how they can be improved. Examine the possible ways of proffering solutions to the needs and choose the most appropriate. Think through your papers; don't assume in your head. There are four basic tests your ideas should pass: value customers enjoy, the chances of the product surviving in the market, the degree of innovation, and the profitability of the business.

Taiwo: Wow! You just blew my mind with your submission. Even though one can't accurately predict future occurrences, there are things one can do to reduce the risk of failure and guarantee success in life.

Collins: Exactly my point; a student who desires to become a doctor must be adequately informed on the O' level subjects he will need to pass, the subject combination he must write in JAMB, the institutions that best teach the course. All this information will guide his decision rightly and increase his chances of becoming a doctor. When a man wants to venture into business, the more information he has about the business environment is a determinant of the success of the business. Information on people's needs, the likely cost of making the product, and the financial strength of his target customers are considered. It will reduce his chances of making the wrong choices in business.

Taiwo: So thoughtful of you; I never reasoned it that way. I need to get back to the drawing board and carry out more research then. I must confess that I was about to venture into the business blindly.

Collins: But I thought you said you have carried out the feasibility studies for your business idea. All this information should have been included in your report.

Taiwo: I actually carried out a miserly feasibility study hoping that Andy would assist me professionally, but I was more engrossed with the business plan.

Collins: This is why it is good to share your ideas with trusted friends, professionals, experts, successful entrepreneurs, and even potential customers where you will be able to get some tips on how to improve your ideas, get more clarification on your assumptions, be ready to accept constructive criticism to bring the best out of your ideas and reduce the risk you incur.

CHAPTER 45

You Can't Please Everybody in Business

Taiwo: My friend, dealing with people can be very frustrating; some people have a way of provoking you.

Collins: So, are you just realizing that human beings are the most difficult of God's creatures to understand and to please? You can't please everybody, which is why one has to embrace patience and tolerance. If not, they can make you commit suicide.

Taiwo: I am telling you. *Imagine someone will ask you to give them five cups of rice while you are measuring it; they will not talk. After you have finished, they will now say, please make it 4; some will ask for a particular brand of noodles. After you have given them the particular brand, they will ask you to change it.* The most annoying one was a customer who came to buy plenty of things from me after wasting my time packing those items, spent more than fifteen minutes haggling the price, and said he wasn't buying again; I felt like cursing him.

Collins: You mean he first haggled the price with you for fifteen minutes, after which you agreed and went to pack the items, only for him to say he wasn't buying again?

Taiwo: Yes, if not more. To make matters worse, there were a few of the items that were not in stock that day. I had to send a boy to help get them from the store, but after all, he didn't buy them.

Collins: Well, that is one of the challenges we face in business; some will order a thing only for them to change their mind after you have bought and sent it to them. You just reminded me of that *House of Ajebo's* skit titled *Aboki*, where the customer asked the Mallam, the seller, to add Geisha, Sardines, Eggs, and Carrots in the largest bread only for him to ask the Mallam to sell ₦10 portion from the entire mix.

Taiwo: *(Taiwo laughs)* Funny when you aren't the one facing such a customer. But you are right, my friend; you can't just please everybody; one must just be patient and embrace tolerance.

Collins: Trying to please everybody is the beginning of insanity, my friend. A man who tries to please everybody ends up displeasing himself. That reminds me of a song by Chief Ebenezer Obey titled '*The man, his son and his donkey.*' Sure, you have heard the song before.

Taiwo: No, what's the song about?

Collins: Really? He sang the song back in 1976; though it is old, it has inspiring lyrics. There was this man who had a donkey. One day, he decided to go out with his son, so they both set out on the donkey. They met a man who called them wicked for both sitting on the donkey at the same time. He then decided to make the son walk while he sat on the donkey alone. Along the way, they met another man who accused him of being selfish for allowing his son to walk while he was on the donkey; he decided to come down from the donkey and made his son sit on the donkey while he walked. After a few meters, they met yet another man who called him a fool for making his child sit on the donkey while he walked. He got tired and decided both he and his son would walk alongside the donkey; just a bit further down the road, they met yet another man who called them slaves for not utilizing the donkey for transport. Then the man looked up and said to himself, there is nothing you can do to please human beings.

Taiwo: Wow! Seriously, that sums it up. I like that insightful song; it's deep. You cannot just please people.

Collins: Yes, you just do your own with a sincere and clear conscience. Personal taste varies; people can change at any time; some are unstable, some are confused, and some don't have a mind of their own, so you just factor all sets of people in business so as not to be provoked to the point of having hypertension.

Taiwo: You are very right; people can make you hypertensive in business if care is not taken. They will make you shout unnecessarily. Another painful thing is when customers you have treated well stop buying from you and start buying elsewhere.

Collins: Expect such kind of people in business. Those are people they call *'Ari iyawo ko iya ile', those* who, because of the new bride, forget their old wife. Such is common; that is why you must be dynamic, stay relevant in business, and maintain good customer relations; those who will stay will stay, and those who can't will not; you are not sent to everybody. Everybody cannot like you, no matter how good you are. One man's food is another man's poison. Some will prefer Coca-Cola to Pepsi-Cola any day, some will prefer Pepsi-Cola to Coca-Cola any day, and some will later change their taste.

Taiwo: Thanks, K. man, for always being there for me.

CHAPTER 46

Advertising/Marketing

Chidi: Hello, children.

Chisom: Hey! Wonders will never end!

Femi: Help me ask your bro! Who are your children here now?

Chidi: You guys, of course. You are my offspring in this business matter. So, how has the branding of the business been?

Femi: Better you are referring to business matters. Business has been dull. We haven't had much patronage since we started.

Chidi: Are you kidding me? But you guys are trendy on Campus.

Chisom: Yes, oh, but they have already gotten used to taking their work to the University's official business centre.

Chidi: I can relate to what you are saying. I did all my design and printing there while I was in school, and those people disappointed me a whole lot. But can I ask you a few questions?

Chisom: No doubts. Go ahead with your questions.

Chidi: Are you sure you have brought your business to the notice of students in your faculty, department, and even your colleagues?

Femi: Well, I only told a few of my coursemates. Why did you ask?

Chidi: No wonder! You have not done much to advertise, publicize, sensitize, create awareness and market your business. The soul of any business is advertisement.

Chisom: Bros, take it easy with all these your sizes...

Chidi: The concept of advertising is to inform, persuade, convince, and appeal to the emotions of potential buyers to buy. I was expecting that you guys would have leveraged your popularity in school, your ability to print well-designed posters, the social media platforms, the school media house, a database containing staff emails, and stuff like that to make your business known to people. You can also customize the T-shirts and the tops you wear to classes to promote your business.

Chisom: Hmm…, I have told a few friends, though, hoping they would help me inform others, but I guess that is not good enough.

Chidi: Yes, that is absolutely not enough. You need to strategize on ways to inform and draw people's attention to what you do. Remember, advertisement is the fertilizer that makes a business grow. Generally speaking, even if it is just a banner, signpost, cardboard advert, or face-to-face advertisement, just ensure it is bold and convincing. One can also promote his business in newspapers and journals. Magazines, radio, TV, movie theatres, billboards, telephone, via the internet, car stickers, exhibitions, trade fairs, etc., but note that your packaging is also a form of advert, so make sure your label, cover, and container are catchy and attractive.

Femi: Thank you so much for sharing your ideas with us, our business daddy.

CHAPTER 47

ICT in Business/E-Business

Titi: Indeed, this world is now a global village. Imagine I just spoke with my elder brother in Australia via the WhatsApp video call; it was as if we were talking to each other physically, even though he is thousands of miles away from here.

Joan: You can say that again. Technology, I mean ICT, has changed the way everything is done. All my dad does now is use his phone to contact a UBER driver to come and pick us up from school.

Titi: Imagine, most times, my mum orders our electronic gadgets from *Jumia.ng* she places the order, and they are delivered to our doorstep. Even this morning, she ordered the cake she wanted to give her aunt for her birthday and sent it to her through TAXIFY.

Idowu: That is what our business studies teacher called E-commerce and E-trade. Our teacher once told us that online business is the way to go because we are now in the digital and information age. Many business owners will not need a physical shop/office because they can transact from the comfort of their homes. All they need to do is place their advert on social media platforms such as WhatsApp, Instagram, Facebook, etc., and have a standby dispatch rider who can help out with the delivery of the ordered items.

Titi: I agree with you because my sister once made a sale of over ₦10,000 in a day on social media. You don't have to be with the buyer of your product; all you need is to receive the order and find a way to send it to the person who then credits your account.

Joan: Indeed, technology has helped entrepreneurs reduce the money they spend on advertising their products or services. They don't necessarily have to go to conventional traditional media houses such as TV stations, radio stations, and newspapers to advertise their products.

Titi: On social media, all you need is your data/subscription, except if you want to use other methods such as Google ads or blogging sites to promote your products, where you will pay a small amount of money. Interestingly, you can reach broader and wider coverage via your social media. I learned there are ways you can generate traffic and make your products visible to lots of people across the world.

Joan: Only that one has to be careful because there are many fake and dubious people online.

Titi: You are right. The famous cybercriminals are called Yahoo-yahoo. Well, you know everything has its advantages and disadvantages.

Idowu: You are both right; indeed, online business is the way to go in this era; any business that doesn't have an online presence is dead on arrival. But come to think of it, ICT is not only about trading or placing adverts on social media; one can also leverage the various demands of ICT by developing these skills. Demands for websites and video animation developers, graphics designers, professional copywriters, internet marketers, computer programmers, and other computer professionals are on the rise daily. One can quickly acquire any of these skills, don't you think?

Joan: Sure, though I never thought along that line, and I have been neglecting computer classes. I need to take it seriously now and enroll in computer training on a weekend basis. Seriously, this is an eye-opener; I have only been using my brother's laptop to play games and watch movies.

Idowu: I used to be like that until I saw the way my neighbours make money on the internet through FOREX trading, internet marketing, and other genuine means and the way my elder brother makes money through his computer skills by designing websites for companies and writing programs. I can tell you the prospects in the field of ICT are enormous since everybody is embracing it, and many business opportunities lie there.

Joan: You made me remember the story of a nine-year-old boy who has developed over 30 computer games all because his dad teased him for playing other people's games instead of thinking of when he will start his own.

Idowu: Instead of watching videos online and helping the likes of Mark-angel comedy and Linda Ikeji make more money, we can equally start using that same internet to make money too.

Titi: Every profession is now going digital and computerized, be it medicine, farming, teaching, trading, accounting, and even the legal profession. So, Joan, you had better start taking your computer classes more seriously.

CHAPTER 48

Endorsement in Business

Bolu: Titi, I am finding it hard to convince people to buy my product. I don't even know what else to do.

Titi: The first thing is, are people aware of your products?

Bolu: I only informed some people about it since my business has not grown to the point of placing an advertisement on radio and TV.

Titi: Have you used online platforms? I mean social media like WhatsApp, Facebook, Twitter, Instagram, etc.

Bolu: I tried sometime back, but I have not been all out with that.

Titi: Okay, have you considered getting an endorsement for your business?

Bolu: Endorsement? You mean getting a celebrity to feature in my jingle or advert? You must be kidding me. I just told you I don't have the resources to go to the radio or TV stations for adverts; you are now talking about getting an endorsement from a celebrity.

Titi: *(Smiles)*Thank God you know the role an endorsement plays on a product when people see a celebrity endorsing a product. It automatically appeals to people's emotions and encourages them to buy their products. This is why many manufacturers seek the endorsement of celebrities and respected people in society. Even authors get the signatures of renowned authors or great figures in society to comment on their books, which appeal to potential buyers.

Bolu: I agree, but at my level, how do I get celebrity endorsements?

(Sister Loveth walks in)

Titi: Ah! Sis Loveth, you are back home for the weekend! I have missed you. Welcome!

Loveth: Afternoon Titi and Bolu! How was school today?

Titi: School was fine. In fact, you walked in at the right moment. How were you able to get Bisola of *Big Brother 9ja* to endorse your perfume business on social media?

Loveth: This girl, won't you even allow me to rest first? Anyway, let me answer you because of your friend. Everybody wants value for their money, so when they see someone of high reputation or honour in society approving a product, their perception or judgment is influenced. So, you don't need to wait until you have money to get the endorsement of a celebrity; you can start by getting the approval or support of somebody known in society who is respected and honoured within your locality. For example, you may use your local church pastor, the Imam in your mosque, the principal of your school, and your local government area chairman to promote your brand on their social media platforms. Or through interacting with their immediate environment, which can go a long way in framing the mindset of potential buyers about your product. You never can tell who these people are connected to.

Bolu: Wow! In that case, I can easily talk to the proprietress; I know she encourages us to be innovative and can help me use her position and influence to promote this.

Loveth: As for me, I got Bisola to help influence my business by messaging her through her social media handle.

Titi: Exactly my point.

CHAPTER 49

Patenting in business

Bola: I can see you are busy with this your innovation. Have you considered getting a patent right for it?

Tolu: Wait, what did I hear you say? Patient right or parent, right? I am working on a combat robot; I am not working on a hospital project; neither am I doing this for my parents.

Bola: *(Smiles)* Don't get it twisted; I didn't say patient or parent. I said patent right.

Tolu: So, what do you mean by that?

Bola: Well, a patent is an official document that says that one person or company has the right to make or sell a new INVENTION or product and that no one else is allowed to copy it. Early patenting is recommended, especially in the case of new products or processes. This will prevent imitators, pirates or other people from stealing your ingenuity or copy it without your permission. The future success of your business can depend on a patent, and in every industry, there are powerful competitors with the means to keep an unfavourable patent from being granted.

Tolu: Wow! That is very necessary, especially in this country of ours, that people can steal other people's work or ideas that years of labour and hard work have gone into to present it as theirs.

Bola: That is the main reason why an inventor and an author need to get patent rights and copyrights for their work or idea.

Tolu: Thank you so much for informing me about this. How do I get this patent?

Bola: One can get the advice of experienced patent lawyers. Some degree of caution is advised because a patent can also miss the mark. In making your innovation or invention public, you still need to protect the composition of the idea so that it will not be improved upon and thus thwarted by others. The recipe for Coca-Cola, for example, is still a secret and has never been patented because the patent can be circumvented with very few neutral-tasting changes.

Tolu: This sounds great!

Bola: Yes, note, one can sign a Confidentiality agreement with your lawyers, venture capitalists, professional consultants, and all other players who are privy to one's innovation or invention. This helps in keeping things under wraps and keeps "poaching" of ideas at bay.

Tolu: But how will I be able to afford a good lawyer's services, or where will I get one?

Bola: That is not difficult. Have you forgotten that Bimpe's dad is a lawyer? Besides, our youth pastor in the church is a lawyer, and he's always interested in seeing youths come up with great ideas and innovations. Some of my dad's friends are lawyers as well.

Bola: You are right; I never thought well about that. I have an uncle who is even a lawyer.

Tolu: But note. Your best protection against intellectual property theft is probably to implement your plan as quickly as possible. A great deal of work must be done between dreaming up an idea and opening for business. This effort called the entry barrier, can keep potential copycats at bay because, in the end, crossing the finish line first makes you the winner, not having the fastest shoes.

CHAPTER 50

Networking

Titi: Hello, Ronke, how are you this morning?

Ronke: Hi, I am very fine. You?

Titi: I am good. I saw your mum and your younger sister at sister Kenny's wedding yesterday, but you weren't there.

Ronke: Yes, I didn't feel like going; I am not the party type.

Titi *(Smiles)*: I have noticed something about you; you don't like to mingle or relate with people. Even in the church, after the grace in fellowship, you pick up your bags and go straight to your Dad's car. At school, you only relate to three people: Joan, Bolu, and me.

Ronke: My sister, too many cooks spoil the broth; the same applies to keeping too many friends. I don't really like to mingle with many people because humans can be funny; I'm sure you can relate. When you start keeping a multitude of friends, you also attract enemies, haters, and pretenders. Not everyone who smiles with you actually wishes you well. I better maintain my circle of three tested and trusted friends.

Titi: I quite agree with you. There are many unfriendly friends, those who speak well about you when you are there but speak ill of you in your absence, and those who are only after what they can get from you.

Ronke: Exactly! I call them parasites!

Titi: *(Smiles)* Funny you, but you know some people come our way as a lesson and some as a blessing; we all need one another, and no one can stand alone. Right from the moment we leave our mum's womb to when we die and are buried in the tomb, we need people. I mean a good relationship with people.

Ronke: No doubt about that, which is why I still have the three of you in my life.

Titi: That is true. It still doesn't mean you can't have acquaintances and be more involved in social gatherings you find yourself.

Ronke: Social gatherings? Parties and the likes? Are parties not just about the food? I can get more than enough at home.

Titi: *(Smiles)* Well, attending parties is not just about the food but about the people you can meet and the relationships you can start that could be beneficial to you in the future. Don't mind me; it's the entrepreneur in me talking to you now, and I know you are also one.

Ronke: Wait, I like that part; how can parties help out in my business? I have some beads and some items I want to sell, but I have yet to find buyers.

Titi: You see exactly what I am saying. In parties or social gatherings like that, you'll meet with people, network with them, and form great business relationships. Just one friend who knows what you do can easily connect you to others who need your products and services. Could you believe that my mum introduced me to a few of her friends yesterday and when they asked what I do, I told them I am into baking and showed them some of my work on the phone. Five of them have already indicated interest in my small chops and cakes. Also, a lady who ate the mince pie (*meat pie*) and *Zobo* I supplied during a program has recommended me to her colleagues.

Ronke: No wonder your business is booming.

Titi: Yes, it is God's grace, but God will not come down from above; He will send people. Your network determines your net worth. You are as strong as the people around you.

Ronke: But you know I am the shy and introverted type of person.

Titi: Yes, I know. To overcome that, you need to inculcate a greeting culture now; when you see people, you need to show respect and courtesy. Smiling can open and soften the hearts of people towards you, and this makes it easy to share your products and services with them. Even when you don't know them, or they look younger, smile and greet them. Try to compliment people sincerely and show appreciation; don't be ashamed or discouraged by the reactions of some because they will ignore you. Another thing that can help you build interpersonal skills is to think of how you can add value to people. Don't be proud, cocky or arrogant when you relate with people; humility is key, and try to relate with your classmates, seniors, juniors, teachers, church members, neighbours, etc. Because they may be potential customers and of help to you in the future.

Ronke: No wonder when I greeted Tolu yesterday, she came to play with me during break today.

Titi: Yes, there is more to networking in business, though; you still get to share ideas with people, and from there, get new ideas on how to expand your business, get to know what is trending and other complementing areas of business you can venture into. But in all, one must still be careful and not jump into any relationship; there are people with selfish motives who want to just take advantage of you.

Ronke: That is the thing. There are many fake people everywhere.

Titi: No doubt about that, but then I believe it is mainly the greedy and covetous that are more prone to deception. In mingling, you also need to define the terms and set boundaries, especially with the opposite sex and maintain some decorum levels. Let people earn your trust before.

Ronke: You are correct; one can't say because there are bad people out there, one will not relate with people; there is a saying that when we close our eyes for evil people to pass, we will not know when good people will pass. Thanks, friend. I owe you one neckpiece.

Titi: Now you get the gist.

Ronke: Wow! Titi, *I never saw it like this before, see how I have been missing free opportunities.* So, social gatherings can be this beneficial to one's business? I have to adjust to that; Solo life does not pay an entrepreneur.

CHAPTER 51

Create Room for Feedback

Femi: *(Ranting on the phone)* Please don't you ever call me again! Good riddance to bad rubbish!

Chisom: *Haba*! My friend, take it easy; who were you ranting with over the phone like that?

Femi: *(Still fuming) Who cares? One negative-minded person who will never appreciate one's effort to satisfy them.*

Chisom: I can see the person must have provoked you greatly. Whatever the person must have done, just take it easy; it is too early to allow somebody to spoil your day for you.

Femi: *Can you imagine the bad belle* telling me that the T-shirt we customized for his company was not good enough and that the prints were peeling off? And to imagine that I complained about the fabric of the T-shirt materials when he brought the job. He gave me the go-ahead himself, saying that they have always used the same material for their customized shirts. *Mtchew!*

Chisom: *So, the person you are venting about is even our customer?*

Femi: Who cares? He has ceased to be a customer because I will never collect a job from him again!

Chidi: Calm down, *biko*. Now, let me ask you a question: After the person complained about your prints, what else did he say about them?

Femi: I guess he must have said that it is that same material they have always been using for their customized uniform, and they have never experienced this kind of issue, so there has to be something their former printer is doing right. We are not getting... I didn't hear him well because I was already provoked; I was expecting somebody who would commend my efforts, not condemn them.

Chidi: I can now understand; let me be honest with you, my dear. There is what is called constructive criticism. Can you see every part of your body?

Femi: Well, I cannot see my back. Why did you ask?

Chidi: Good, you see, nobody can see it all, no matter how sharp your eyes or vision can be. Nobody is an island; nobody is God, who is Omniscient and all-knowing. We must be able to embrace constructive criticism by putting a feedback mechanism in place. You see, no one likes his or her work to be condemned. We all feel good when our efforts are commended, but the truth is that we grow better and stronger through constructive criticism. Why do you always check the mirror after dressing up? Is it not to point you to areas you need to adjust on your face or dressing? That is exactly what constructive criticism does; it helps you see the areas you need to work on so that your business can do better.

Chisom: Hmm...

Chidi: So, I don't want you to see it that way when some people talk about your product in a way you don't like; see it as a way to improve on it and make it better. Some will speak to condemn you rightly, some will speak to commend you, while some will criticize and share tips to improve on it, and I think this person belongs to the last category. I believe he was simply challenging you to improve on your current printing technologies.

Chisom: True. We actually used a Stencil approach to customize the shirts. Though we have also talked about getting the latest technology in printing, which is 3-dimensional, we haven't made enough profit to purchase it.

Chidi: The appropriate thing that should have been done in this case is to take the printing aspect of the job to a printer with the machine that can give you the best result. If you have had a good rapport with other experienced printers and have been giving room for feedback, you would have known the right technological approach to use on such fabrics. Let there be an avenue to receive feedback from your customers; it will help you know what they really want and how best you can serve them; after all, we are in business for them.

Femi: Ah... I have just lost a customer, and probably the referral that we might have gotten through him.

Chidi: All hope is not lost yet. You can still call back the customer to apologize and discuss what can be done so that both parties will be happy. And I hope you have learned not to be rude to a customer. Be patient, listen to what they have to say, and process it well before responding.

Femi: Let me quickly call him back. He is still our customer.

CHAPTER 52

Customer Retention

Femi: *(On the phone with the irate customer)* Good afternoon, Mr. Marcus

Mr. Marcus: Why are you calling me? Have you called to continue insulting me?

Femi: No, on the contrary, I have called to apologize for my earlier actions.

Mr. Marcus: I don't have time for this; I am a very busy man.

Femi: Please, sir. I sincerely apologize. I was in a bad frame of mind, and it was just a case of transferred aggression. Please forgive me, sir.

Mr. Marcus: Ah! Femi, you really made me feel bad. You made me regret bringing the business to you. I would have taken it to my other printer but for Chisom's enthusiasm and persistence. This is my first trial with you guys, you know?

Femi: Yes, sir, I realized I was wrong. I shouldn't have reacted that way.

Mr. Marcus: I was only trying to inform you that there are ways you could have done the job better than this. After all, it is the same material my former printer has been printing on, and we have never experienced this.

Femi: I would have seen the good in your constructive criticism if I had calmly listened and reasoned with you. I assure you, I have learnt my lesson, and this will never happen again.

Mr. Marcus: Okay. No problem. It has passed, and I have forgiven you.

Femi: Please, can those T-shirts be returned so we can rectify the mistakes we made?

Mr. Marcus: Is that even possible? There's no need for that. That particular set of shirts was even for our IT students. They will leave after six months.

Femi: Hope this will not affect our business relationship, sir?

Mr. Marcus: Oh, not at all. You have done what most people wouldn't do. You impressed me with your ability to accept your wrongs and correct your mistakes.

Femi: I assure you that we will give you a special concession and rebate when you contact us for a job next, and this time, it will be very well done because we are going digital now.

Mr. Marcus: (*Laughing*) That's a deal then. My regards to Chisom.

Femi: Okay, sir. Enjoy the rest of your day, sir. (*Ends the call*)

Chisom: That went quite well. I can see you smiling now.

Femi: Yes, oh. I really provoked him, but we are cool now. Thank you, our business, Daddy.

Chidi, I would have made us lose such a nice customer.

Chidi: You are welcome, my business baby.

CHAPTER 53

Follow-Up Your Clients/ Customers

(Mr. Marcus pays a visit to Chisom and Femi in their shop)

Mr. Marcus: Good morning, my special friend Femi and the most persistent businessman I know, Chisom. I can see you guys have really upgraded and gone digital, like you said.

Femi & Chisom: (*Laughing*) Good morning, Mr Marcus.

Chisom: Yes, sir. It is to satisfy you, our esteemed and distinguished customers. Wow! We are so happy to see you this morning.

Femi: Despite all that happened, you still came back. You just made my day. Thank you, sir!

Mr. Marcus: Don't mention; it's bygone now.

Chisom: Mr Marcus, to what do we owe this your pleasant morning surprise? Anything for your boys?

Mr. Marcus: (*Laughs*) Chisom and money? Well, I brought a job for you. You will help me print 250 copies of a Calendar and another 250 copies of Diaries so I can share them with my customers as New Year souvenirs.

Femi: Okay, sir. Let me bring samples so you can make your choice. Or do you have any particular specifications in mind?

Mr. Marcus: No, please let me take a look at your samples. (*Checks the samples and makes his choice*) I like these designs. How much will they cost?

Femi: The total cost should be ₦150,000, but we will be doing it for you at ₦130,000 because we must keep our promise.

Mr. Marcus: Good! I trust I will have my consignments in two weeks at the latest. And I hope it will be done well, as promised.

Chisom: You can rest assured, sir, that you will get the very best.

Mr. Marcus: Nice doing business with you.

(A month later)

Chisom: *(Places a call through to Mr Marcus)* Good morning, sir. Compliments of the season to you, our MVC-most valuable customer!

Mr. Marcus: A very good morning to you, too, my good friend! Compliment of the season to you, too! How are you and the family?

Chisom: Fine, thank God, sir. I believe you and the family are fine, too. I actually called with respect to our last delivery. I hope you and your customers really like the Calendars and the Diaries.

Mr. Marcus: Thank you so much for checking on the work you did. It's quite unusual with other artisans and service providers I have worked with. Most don't bother to find out about their clients and customers if they enjoy their services or products. I am highly impressed.

Chisom: Thank you, sir. That is part of our business culture; customers' satisfaction is our pleasure. We try to make sure our customers enjoy value for their money, sir.

Mr. Marcus: You guys actually surpassed my expectations. The quality of the work is superb, and my customers have been commending the design and printing. In fact, that reminds me, two of my friends who run school businesses have complained about the lackadaisical attitudes of their printers. I will recommend you guys to them.

Chisom: *(Smiling)*Thank you so much, sir, we will surely appreciate that.

Mr. Marcus: That's the beauty of you checking on your customers; if not for the fact that you called now, I wouldn't have remembered my friends needed a new printer, and I wouldn't have recommended you. Once we end this call now, I will surely put a call through to them.

Chisom: You see why you are our most valuable customer? Thanks a lot, sir. May God bless you. Bye!

Femi: Who did you speak to that is making you smile like someone who just won a jackpot? I know it must be a woman.

Chisom: You and women matter; this is business. You remember your special customer, Mr. Marcus?

Femi: Yes.

Chisom: I decided to follow up with him to see how he is enjoying our product and services; he felt so happy that we could check him up and decided to connect us to his friends who are school owners and have been complaining about their printers.

Femi: Wow! That is a big one! Following up, customers and clients are actually part of business ethics, only that many shy away from it. They are usually scared of incurring additional costs on calls or knowing that the quality of what they have done is poor, and some just think it is not important.

CHAPTER 54

Business Registration

Chidi: Hope you guys have registered your business?

Chisom: With the school authority?

Chidi: No, I mean with the Corporate Affairs Commission (C.A.C.)!

Femi: No, we haven't done that.

Chidi: But why?

Chisom: Well, we hope to do that when the business grows big enough.

Chidi: You guys are making a costly mistake which can affect you later on.

Femi: Is business registration that serious at this infant stage? I think registering a business at this early stage will affect its financial stability. Before you know it, tax authorities will be demanding that we remit part of our profits that could be used to strengthen our capital base.

Chidi: I see. So, it is the payment of tax that is scaring you from doing what is needed. Have you considered the cost and risks of not registering your business early? It will shock you that what you stand to gain by registering your business, invention, and product with the necessary agencies is more than what you stand to sacrifice.

Chisom: Can you please shed some light on the need for business registration?

Chidi: The truth is that you may be building something that could become very big and popular in the future; however, if you don't do something as basic as registering your business, all your efforts and hard work can easily be wasted or, worse, taken over by another. Registering your business gives you the legal right to operate. It also protects your business brand and gives you a unique identity.

Femi: Hmm.

Chidi: Let me give you an instance. Imagine a guy by the name of John Paul has a clothing line but is not registered. John Paul, being very good at his craft, made beautiful and quality clothes, which attracted many customers. Simon Fraud was in the same business as John Paul but not as good as him, which made him record lower patronage. He discovered that John Paul hadn't registered his business, so he went ahead and registered his business and brand with John Paul. This made his sales shoot up. By the time John Paul found out, he had sued him, but it was too late; the only option for him was to register his business with another name, which might affect the brand he had laboured to build.

Chisom: That's wickedness.

Chidi: Well, that was morally wrong but legally right. This is just one of the reasons why you need to register your business. Your business can be registered as a Sole proprietorship if it is just one man's affairs. You can register it as a partnership, just like what you guys are doing. You can register it as a limited liability company under which you have a public limited liability company (P.L.C.) and a private limited liability company (L.T.D.). All of them have their advantages and disadvantages.

Femi: Boss, apart from the legal covering business registration comes with, does it provide other benefits?

Chidi: Sure, though it depends on the business structure. Registering your business protects you from personal liabilities and risks, especially if you are registered as a limited liability company. It makes you look serious and attracts more customers. It makes it easier for you to secure bank loans and credit facilities. It helps you attract investors. Another reason why business registration is important is that it promotes continuity. Interestingly, the process of registering your business has been made simple. You don't need the services of an expert; you can visit the C.A.C. website, fill in your business details, and pay the required amount to the bank.

Chisom: It is good to have a mentor from whom one can always get adequate information and direction. I have only been dwelling on the theoretical side of what I have been taught without the practical aspect.

Femi: You are right. No more procrastination; we have to get our business registered.

CHAPTER 55

Endurance/Perseverance in Business

Mariam: You seem to be excited this morning; what could be the secret?

Ngozi: *(Smiles)*My mum decided to give us a special treat this morning, and she has also promised to take us to recreation centres this weekend.

Mariam: Wow! I am happy for you guys.

Ngozi: Thanks, friend.

Mariam: Is she celebrating her birthday, or what are you guys celebrating?

Ngozi: No, she is not celebrating her birthday; she just decided to appreciate God and the family for persevering with her all the time. Her business was faced with lots of challenges, and she almost felt like giving up. Today, her business is growing and booming, and she now has lots of customers.

Mariam: Wow! I am so happy for your mum, but the reverse has been the case for mine; she has complained about low sales. Sometimes, she doesn't makeup to ₦2,000 in a day in her business. It is quite frustrating.

Ngozi: My friend, I can relate to what you are saying. Did you hear why I said Mum decided to give us a wonderful treat? She, too, had experienced a similar situation. One of the virtues that I have learned from Mum and that has also helped me is her resilience and perseverance in business. There were times I followed her to her shop, and for hours, nobody would even come in to ask for what we had, let alone buy what we sold. There were times she felt like giving up; in fact, some friends even advised her to pick up a paid job and close down the shop. Thank God she didn't give up. See how far her business has grown now.

Mariam: Hmm… I just pray things will turn around for the better in my mum's business, too.

Ngozi: Amen. Just keep encouraging her that things will soon turn around for her good; I remember the story of Colonel Sander, who tried to license his fried chicken recipe but was rejected more than 1006 times. I even read a book by Donald Trump, where he shared how he experienced a major setback in his business but was able to bounce back because he didn't give up. Let me leave you with this quote from Sam Adeyemi: *'Successful people are the failures that refuse to quit while failures are successful people that quit easily.'* Remember the story of Thomas Edison, who experimented hundreds of times before inventing the bulb?

Mariam: Yes, I do. I like that quote; I will surely write and paste it in a conspicuous place for Mum to see. I remember the story of a woman who has built two houses in our area from his bean cake business. Even though she is old now, one of her children currently manages the business with more than ten workers. She shared her story with us on how she trained 4 of her children in the university from the *'Akara'* business. She told us it wasn't easy at first, but with patience, resilience, and tenacity, God has prospered her.

Ngozi: That's it!

CHAPTER 56

Stay Positive and be Optimistic

Hassan: Why were you and Usman shouting at each other the other time? I have always known the two of you to be good friends.

Ibrahim: Hassan, don't mind him; he finds it hard to heed to advice. Any time you advise him, he will make sure he opposes it; he acts like Mr. Know it all.

Hassan: I Hope you guys have been able to resolve the whole matter?

Ibrahim: *Well, I have left him to his decision; anything he likes, let him do.*

Hassan: *Uhm!* This matter must really be a serious matter. What could have triggered the fracas?

Ibrahim: *My brother, don't mind him; the thing is, he wants to use his savings to buy fruits from his neighbour who has an orchard and be supplying the woman selling fruits close to the school gate.*

Hassan: *Ahan! Ahan!* But that's a noble idea, so what's the big deal there?

Ibrahim: Well, I advised him not to do so.

Hassan: But why? What are your reasons?

Ibrahim: I know a man who once tried that business but ended up in debt, and I also know that Usman doesn't have the time. He can actually use the money to do other things, and besides, it is a risky venture. He hasn't considered if the woman will buy into his idea. What if he runs into a loss? What if the business doesn't work out? What if his parents and school management find out? There are so many negative occurrences that surround the execution of the idea. We just have to be realistic here. I believe this business isn't right for him.

Hassan: Oh! I can see you really care about your friend. You don't want him to fail and lose his money, but it seems his mind is made up, and you can't talk him out of it.

Ibrahim: Exactly! I know if this doesn't work out, he will come back to me to bail him out, and besides, the school might suspend him if they get to know, and his parents would be angry with me for supporting such.

Hassan: I see… Ibrahim, but you know there are always two sides to a coin. Have you tried to see it the other way around?

Ibrahim: What is the other way?

Hassan: The positive way, of course! What if his parents supported the idea and encouraged his thoughtfulness? What if the school management wouldn't kick against it since they support entrepreneurship? What if the woman gladly embraces the idea because it will relieve her of the stress of going to the market herself? What if the business succeeds? After all, we all like fruits. What if he makes profits since he would be buying at a very cheap rate from the orchard? Well, life is all about risk; it is a 50/50 thing. We just have to focus on the positive outcomes, too, which is the Big Picture, instead of always dwelling on the likely negative outcomes.

Ibrahim: Hmm… I quite agree with you; thanks for opening my eyes to another way of seeing it. See him under the tree; I hope you wouldn't mind following me to go and apologize and strategize on how to go about it to reduce the likely risk involved.

Hassan: Okay.

CHAPTER 57

Avoid Negative People

Ibrahim: Usman.

Usman: What's it?

Hassan: *Haba!* Usman, are you still angry with your friend?

Usman: What friend? How can someone who doesn't want my progress be my friend? How can you call someone who doesn't see any good in any idea I bring forward? Someone who believes his own way is the only right way. Someone who constantly kills any business idea I come up with and talks me out of it. I once shared a business idea of selling stationery in school with him, but he discouraged me; the same thing happened when I suggested that we go to the cobbler's shop so we could learn how to make and mend shoes.

Hassan: I can see you are really angry.

Usman: Yes. I have had enough of his negative, cynical, and pessimistic attitude. See! I have made up my mind not to give room for bad energies in my life again and let everybody go their separate ways; after all, we don't bear the same name.

Ibrahim: *Haba!* It hasn't gotten to this.

Usman: It has, in fact, it has even gone beyond this. You see, I have made up my mind to start this business, and I don't want someone to talk me out of it again. In case you don't know, I have already discussed it with the woman in question, and she is very interested; I have already spoken to the Vice-principal about it, and he applauded the idea. He even encouraged me to go ahead since it is not within the school environment and not against the school's regulations. He only advised me not to allow it distract my academics. And for your information, my parents have always encouraged us to start thinking of ways to be financially independent.

Ibrahim: Wow! That's great to hear. So, you have gone this far? I actually came to meet you so we could strategize on how to go about your business idea.

Usman: See who is talking? You mean to strategize how you can use your negative vibes to talk to me out of it again? (*Laughs sarcastically*) I laugh in Swahili.

Hassan: Usman, I commend your strong decision not to entertain negative energy into your space again. With these steps you have taken, I really salute your courage and determination to succeed. In fact, you will go far if you continue like this. However, after the discussion I had with Ibrahim, I realized he didn't mean any harm but was only trying to protect his friend from venturing into what might bring financial losses and heartbreak associated with it. This is why he has actually come here to apologize and strategize with you on ways to go about your business idea. In fact, he specifically requested I follow him.

Usman: Hmm...

Ibrahim: Usman, I am really sorry for my negative dispositions and attempts to rub my fears on you. Hassan has convinced me to view things from the positive side, not only the negative side. I am now a changed man.

Usman: I hear you. You must be kidding me.

Ibrahim: This is for real; my leopard has changed its black spot. Guy, you have really gone far with this business idea. You have really challenged me with the progress you have made in such a short time without me. Now that our business is already on its way to greatness, I am sure I will be the treasurer.

Usman: (*Smiles*). Not only the treasurer, what about being the bank?

Ibrahim: So, I hope we are good to go again?

Usman: Sure! We are 'gees' for life.

Hassan: Now that you guys are back, I hope I will get free fruit supplies by the time you guys start.

Ibrahim: Thanks, Hassan; in fact, you owe me something. Sorry, I mean, I owe you something.

Hassan: Alright, guys, the break is over.

CHAPTER 58

Avoid Complacency

Nuru: Aliko Dangote of our time. Oh boy! You have arrived; see how your business is booming daily.

Usman: It is God, not by my power.

Nuru: At least with this great feat, you can take a break and relax small.

Usman: *(Smiles)*That is a good idea. I doubt if I did that. If I wanted to take a break, it would only be for a few days, and then business would continue.

Nuru: You don't want to give yourself a break?

Usman: You see, there shouldn't be room for complacency in business. I once listened to the story of Dan Lok, who once gave himself a target that by a particular age, he would have become so financially independent that he wouldn't need to work again. Providence smiled at him, and he was able to achieve his goal. He quit his job and went to a nice place for vacation. His plan was just to live in pleasure for the rest of his life. After a few days of holiday, he got tired of it because he was used to working, and he knew there was still more to do.

Nuru: *(Smiles)*I quite agree with you; just by pulling your legs, there is no room to be tired. My dad always tells me how happy and elated he is anytime I take the first position in the class. He also admonishes me not to rest on my oars. He always demands I strive to be better because if I don't, others will overtake me. This has made me always compete with myself, not with others, in order for me to bring out the best in me. If I compare myself with others, I will start running at their pace, which will make me unable to maximize my potential.

Usman: No wonder no one has been able to take the first position from you.

Nuru: *(Smiles)* Usman. I don't know about that; what I know is that to keep being the best, you must always raise your game because there is always room for improvement, no matter the successes you have recorded.

Usman: The same thing applies to business. This is why people like Bill Gates, Mark Zuckerberg, Femi Otedola, and Aliko Dangote do not allow complacency; they still work around the clock, strategize, and diversify into new businesses. Look at Dangote. After exploring the world of sugar, cement, and rice, he moved to other areas of domestic items like salt, seasoning, noodles, pasta, etc., now venturing into the oil industry.

Nuru: That is the spirit. Any truly successful person in life never feels he has arrived and never rests on their oars. They always strike for more and always think of new areas to conquer,

Usman: That is how businessmen think. Thanks, my friend.

CHAPTER 59

Gaining Financial Independence

Taiwo: Good morning, Bimpe. What caused the noise in your house last night? I was scared when I heard your mum on top of her voice.

Bimpe: Hmmm, it was just a heated disagreement between my parents and my elder brother.

Taiwo: You mean Uncle TJ?

Bimpe: Yes

Taiwo: Uncle TJ again? This is becoming unbecoming. Is it the issue of him not being interested in doing anything other than getting a white-collar job?

Bimpe: Yes, we are all tired of him staying at home idle. Though it has been resolved, he finally agreed to learn a vocation.

Taiwo: Thank God for that.

Bimpe: You know what happened prompted many thoughts in me.

Taiwo: Please don't keep me in the dark here.

Bimpe: Well, nothing serious. I just feel I need to start planning my future now and what to do after my education so as not to be like my brother.

Taiwo: Hmm... That is quite deep.

Bimpe: Yes, you see, my brother has been at home for more than 3 years after graduation from the university with nothing to do. He has been on the lookout for jobs since then, but nothing is forthcoming. He's now a frustrated man who picks up fights and gets angry easily. My parents have been advising him to learn a vocational skill, but he insisted he wanted a white-collar job in a bank or oil company. Mum had even suggested once that he should come up with a business idea for her to support him with the capital, but he never came up with something concrete, which frustrated my parents, too.

Taiwo: But I think this country contributed to this in a way; graduates keep trooping out of our higher institutions with no hope of getting a job if they are not connected to high-profile personalities in the country.

Bimpe: Well, you are right in a way, but how long shall we continue to blame this country and depend on it? I think we all need to acquire one skill or another while in school so as not to be dependent on our parents after they have spent a fortune on our education. By the time I am 18, I want to make sure I would have become financially independent of my parents to an extent.

Taiwo: You are very correct; it is quite pathetic seeing some guys close to 40 still depending on their parents to feed them. I decided long ago not to be dependent on my parents or society after graduation, so that's what prompted me to share my foodstuff and provision business idea with my uncle, who is into the business. I also think that is why the government made entrepreneurship studies compulsory for all students in the university.

Bimpe: That is true, but you know many lecturers only read from the book, and many students only read to pass and not to know, let alone apply. But we still need practical experience on how to start and manage a business.

Taiwo: You are correct. I learnt very well from my uncle, who shared his practical business experiences with me. You had better come and enrol in my Business 101 class.

CHAPTER 60

Be Firm and Decisive

Principal: Mr. Jalato, where are your lesson notes and class register records?

Mr. Jalato: Please, sir, I am yet to complete it due to the mid-term exam questions I have been setting.

Principal: You ought to have submitted it since, but I gave you the grace of three weeks. If by next week, you have yet to complete it, I will report you to the proprietress of the school.

Mr. Jalato: Okay, sir. Thank you.

(The sixth week)

Principal: I believe you are through with your lesson note; this is the sixth week.

Mr. Jalato: Please, sir, I tried to finish the note, but...

Principal: No problem. I have tried enough; when the proprietress comes, you can explain it to her.

(Principal reports to the Proprietress)

Proprietress: Mr. Jalato, go and bring your lesson notes.

Mr. Jalato: Yes, ma.

Proprietress: What! You mean you stopped at week 2 when we are in week 6? What have you been using to teach my students? What have I been paying you for? What younger teachers shouldn't be doing is what you are doing.

Mr. Jalato: It's not like that, ma; I have too much on my hands to do and...

Proprietress: Well, I don't have time to waste. I will issue you a query, and you will not receive your salary until your notes are up to date.

Bisi: Mum, why were you so harsh to Mr Jalato? You know he's an old man.

Proprietress: You will not understand, but I will let you understand, you see in business, if you are not firm, some people will take advantage of your simplicity and kindness. This is not his first time, and I have been tolerant enough. You have to maintain your stand for what is right; even when you have to step on toes, you can't please everybody. Some people will come your way to ruin your business. Imagine not writing lesson notes for more than four weeks; what has he been teaching them? You see, you don't mix emotions with business. You must learn to separate business from family, or else they will ruin it. If you condone some things in business, other people will use it against you, and they, too, will start doing it. Before you know it, the business will crumble. So, you have to maintain your stand and not look at their faces. Have good principles you live by. A weakling cannot run a business.

CHAPTER 61

Be Flexible and Dynamic in Business

(Meeting of the executive arm of Balogun market traders' association)

Chidi: Good afternoon, my fellow business tycoons. This is our final quarterly meeting. As you all know, we shall be reviewing our performance in the last quarter, and we shall be having a discussion on the usual end-of-the-year contribution.

Kosini: Thank you for welcoming us, our amiable chairman.

Bukola: Good afternoon, our *Oga at the top.*

Jana: Good afternoon, everybody; sorry for coming a bit late.

Chidi: It's okay. You are welcome. Now that we are all complete, can we move straight to the business of the day? Secretary over to you.

Bukola: *(She reads the minutes of the last meeting, which was adopted by Kosini and seconded by another member of the executive)* Now, regarding the main agenda, we have earmarked some projects to be carried out before the year runs out. These projects include the laying of pipes for the exhaust of traders' generators, the repair of the market restrooms, and the end-of-the-year party. I will now call on the head of the planning committee to give us an update.

Kosini: We have met with the necessary contractors, and the total bill is ₦2,000,000. And as we all know, according to our practice in this place, we share the financial burden among all traders. Based on our calculation, all registered traders will pay ₦3,000 each, while each member of the executive is expected to pay ₦15,000.

Jana: Ah! That is much. It is almost the end of the year, and I cannot afford that; for over two months now, my business has been at a standstill.

Chidi: Really? You mean your business has been at a standstill for that long? But people are still taking photographs, and social events take place every week. I'm aware you used to have at least two events to cover per week before, aside from people who visit your photo studio for photo shoots.

Jana: Hmm... it is not like before. Patronage has been nothing to write home about, and Kosini is even aware.

Kosini: Why won't it be so? When you have refused to be flexible and dynamic in your business. You have always been using the same archaic methods and technology. Technology has left you far behind. Have I not been advising you to be dynamic and flow with the current trend?

Bukola: True; I remember telling her what I saw at an event I went to. The person who covered that event used modern equipment such as drones, digital cameras, etc. I even showed her pictures I took at the event, which were instantly edited and converted to a canvas frame.

Chidi: Which technology are you using, Jana?

Kosini: Don't mind her; she is still using a tripod and analogue cameras that make use of films. You have to wait a minimum of three days before getting a single picture from her studio.

Bukola: Imagine when photographers are already using digital cameras and computers to edit pictures. In her case, she will still go to the darkroom to print pictures, which makes it impossible to edit and filter her pictures.

Chidi: Jana, this is bad. One has to be flexible and dynamic in the business world today, or else one will lose customers. Time is of the essence in business; people want to do business with those who will save them time and give them good quality. Imagine people coming to buy goods worth ₦500,000, and you have to be counting it; all they do is use POS or transfer the money. Even mechanics are now becoming dynamic in their services; they now have scanning devices to scan a car to detect faults and fix them digitally. Banks, network service providers, and even DSTV are all trying to make business easy for their customers now; they provide self-help services.

Jana: Hmm. My customers used to joke with me that I was old school, but I didn't take them seriously.

Bukola: Well, it is not too late; you can enrol in some online training on photography. With your experience on the job, you will soon attract your customers back when they see you have stepped up your game to current technology.

Jana: And to think of it, I was reluctant to come for the meeting. I have been challenged and will surely take it. So, when is the deadline for the contribution payment?

Kosini: Every amount of money is expected to come in by the first week of December to enable the speedy completion of the projects and finalize the planning for our party.

Chidi: At this juncture, I think we need to end this meeting. Who is moving the motion for the adjournment?

(Jana moved the motion for the adjournment while Kosini seconded).

CHAPTER 62

Proactivity in Business

Kenny: Taiwo, I want to buy power oil; take your money. I know you will not give me for free.

Taiwo: I am out of oil; let me quickly get it from my neighbour. I thought the dispatch would bring it for me yesterday, but I guess the rain stopped him from coming. I hope he will bring it this morning.

Kenny: Why is he not yet here? It is already 10 o'clock, other customers might start coming to ask for it now.

Taiwo: I have already called him; he said he's on his way to my shop.

Kenny: But if a customer asks for it now, what will you do?

Taiwo: Don't worry about that; we know how to do it.

Kenny: Okay

(A customer enters)

Customer: Please, do you have vegetable oil?

Kenny: Taiwo, can you see what I was telling you *(She faces the customer)*? Please, we are sorry ma, we don't...

Taiwo: We don't have it yet in the shop; let me quickly help you get it. Can you please give me a few minutes? Please come and have your seat. What other things do you want to buy? We have rice, pepper, garri...

Customer: How much is your garri and rice?

Taiwo: Kenny, please attend to her while I go to get the oil.

(He dashes out to their neighbour's place selling the same products to borrow vegetable oil and returns with it... after the customer has left.)

Kenny: Ah! Taiwo!

Taiwo: Wait, what did you want to tell her when she asked for it?

Kenny: I wanted to tell her you didn't have it so that she can check other shops.

Taiwo: See you, you don't know how to do business. You have to be proactive and think fast when doing business. Imagine if I had told her I didn't have the vegetable oil; she might not have bought the other items from me.

Kenny: But that looks like a lie.

Taiwo: Well, it is just being proactive in business. Technically, she requested oil first, which I didn't have; if I had told her straight away, she might have gone to another shop to get everything. So, because I don't have oil in stock now, I would have lost all the money I just made from her. Let me ask you: if someone wants to give you a contract to supply furniture items to the governor's house, what will you tell him?

Kenny: Well, since I am not into the upholstery business and I am not a carpenter, I will tell him I'm not in such business; if they are convinced enough, they will still give me the job.

Taiwo: I said it; you don't know how to do business. You see, there is nothing wrong with being honest and sincere, but you don't out rightly decline a business offer until after you have exhausted all possible means to get the work done and you have realized it isn't feasible. You need to quickly carry out research on those in the business and make business deals with them. This is what is called outsourcing; this is a form of business on its own. You get contracts, then look for those who will execute them; this is what contractors do.

Kenny: I never looked at it in this light.

Taiwo: That's it; most celebrities who have their clothing lines don't know how to sew; they employ professional tailors who sew and get paid. One has to be proactive in being in business.

Kenny: You are very right. It is not the owner of halogen security that goes about securing clients' facilities; he employs guys who can do it, he collects money from the clients and pays his staff.

Taiwo: Exactly! So, one just has to be proactive to stay in business, or else ignorance will cause one to lose customers God sends one's way.

Kenny: I was sincerely wrong, thanks, twinnie. The boy is already coming with the goods.

CHAPTER 63

Understand The Pocket of Your Customers

Taiwo: Kenny, what happened? That customer who just left doesn't look happy.

Kenny: That's why I don't like anything business; you are really trying. What will one not see in business? You can imagine that lady asking me to sell one tuber of yam for her when it was obvious it was three tubers per stack you arranged and asked me to sell.

Taiwo: But you know fingers are not equal; what Mr. A can afford might not be affordable by Mr. B, so it is business sense to sell to Mr. A yet not deny Mr. B access to what you sell.

Kenny: So, what should I have done?

Taiwo: (*Smiles*) Nice question. Since I told you to sell a stack for ₦900, seeing the willingness of the lady to buy, you could have sold a tuber for her for ₦300.

Kenny: But you didn't tell me that before you left; besides, if I had sold it that way, what would now happen to the remaining two tubers?

Taiwo: Well, in business, we can't predict all the outcomes; we have to be flexible and proactive when making decisions. Anyway, you have never shown interest in business; that's why you haven't heard this story from Uncle John; it would have helped you with this case. He told me how one of his area brothers, working in a company manufacturing a brand of seasoning, gave him cartons of seasonings that had a few weeks to expire to sell. He decided to go to some interior parts of Ibadan to sell them. Some local women couldn't afford a carton, so he decided to sell both in packs and units. All he did was just divide the price of a pack by the number of units inside it; by so doing, he was able to sell more quantity at a faster rate because many of them couldn't afford to buy in packs or cartons but in units.

Kenny. Meaning he was able to achieve more than he would have if he had insisted on selling per carton or pack.

Taiwo: Exactly! His own was to sell the total cartons given to us, any means through which he achieved that doesn't concern the company. The interesting thing is that he gained more money selling in units than selling in packs, and the women were happy because they got it at a lower price than usual, so it was a win-win situation. This is why you see many producers making different sizes of their products so that anyone can buy according to their purse.

Kenny: No wonder. The last time we traveled, they had different categories of boarders on the plane. They have a first-class, business-class, and economy to accommodate everybody. I don't really have any business sense at all; I have a long way to go.

Taiwo: Oh! Oh! Now that you are showing interest in business, you can now see you have lots to learn, you better be ready to stay more with me in my business to learn more practical tips.

CHAPTER 64

Be Meticulous in Business

Taiwo: Kenny, welcome back. How was shopping? I hope Chidi, my supplier, attended to you well.

Kenny: Yes, I met him in the shop and gave him the list. He's such a friendly man; he gave the list to his boys while we discussed it cheerfully.

Taiwo: Okay, please help me attend to customers while I unpack and check through the goods you just brought.

Kenny: Okay.

(Taiwo checks through the goods and notices different variations of Tomato Paste, Spaghetti and sachet oil from what he ordered)

Taiwo: Kenny! But most of these things are different from what I wrote on the list.

Kenny: Like what? Are they not the things you said I should buy that were included?

Taiwo: I specifically wrote the brand of Tomato paste, Spaghetti, and Sachet oil that I need because that's what students buy here and not these.

Kenny: I didn't bother to check for the brand name since I realized the quantity matched the number of items on the list.

(A customer walks in)

Customer: Kenny, I just checked through the change you gave me and realized you gave me excess change.

Kenny: How?

Taiwo: What happened?

Customer: I bought goods worth ₦300 and gave you ₦500. You were supposed to give me ₦200, but you gave me ₦700.

Kenny: Ah! I assumed you gave me a ₦1000 note! You know I was discussing with my brother when you came in.

Taiwo: Thank you very much for your sincerity; not everybody will do this.

(After the customer had left)

Taiwo: See, I was still complaining about the goods you brought, and now another one happened.

Kenny: I'm so sorry.

Taiwo: No problem; next time, just pay close attention to details. What if these items cannot be returned? What if the customer is not honest? You see, one has to be meticulous to stay in business. You pay attention to your customers' needs, to their requests, to the amount given to you, etc. Though nobody is above mistake, you can't afford to constantly make this kind of mistake that could ruin your business. Imagine making a similar mistake of giving the wrong change to ten different people.

Kenny: Ah! That will result in a huge loss. Indeed, there is more to business than I thought. I still have plenty of things to learn. *No, be small thing...*

Taiwo: One step at a time.

CHAPTER 65

Personal Development

Bayo: Which book is that in your hand?

Lolu: It is the Physics 401 textbook.

Bayo: Okay, I thought it was Rich Dad and Poor Dad by Robert Kiyosaki.

Lolu: You and all these your business and motivational books. I hope you know exams will start in a few weeks' time.

Bayo: My dear, after passing the exams, what happens to you? Would you be given a paper certificate and join those looking for white-collar jobs up and down, right? My guy, it is good to prepare for school exams, but how prepared are you for the real examinations out there? It is not enough to go to school; one must be educated.

Lolu: You have started again.

Bayo: What did I start?

Lolu: Which one is schooling, and which one is education? Is it not in school you get an education?

Bayo: (*Smiles*) Well, I quite agree with you that school provides the basic platform for education. Still, there are other avenues through which one can get an education outside the four walls of the school. Besides, not all who graduate from school are really educated. See the way you are looking at me; let me break it down for you.

Lolu: I am all ears.

Bayo: Do you know Bill Gates, Mark Zuckerberg, and Steve Jobs didn't complete their formal schooling before they became entrepreneurs?

Lolu: Are you kidding me?

Bayo: I am not. You see, education is the process of developing and building our mental capacity to make an impact on the society that the school provides. Still, many people are in school not because they want to develop their minds but because they want to have certificates. Having certificates without undergoing mental development and transformation will not do society any good. This is the problem in our society today; there are many graduates, but only a few are educated. Though Bill Gates and the likes mentioned didn't complete their college education, they were able to make tremendous impacts in society because they took time to develop their minds. Don't get me wrong; schooling is very good because it provides the platform to be educated; even Bill Gates and the like saw the need for it and went back to complete their degrees. The essence of schooling is to be educated.

Lolu: I can get your points now. This is why you read other books that you mentioned.

Bayo: Exactly! You see, one must not just limit oneself to academic books but also connect and learn from great minds to develop our minds by reading educational and inspirational books. Personal development is very important in life. There are some things schools will not teach us, such as developing our interpersonal skills, working on our temperament, developing our communication skills, winning the hearts of potential customers, etc.

Lolu: I used to think that if I could finish with good grades in my academics, my success in life would already be guaranteed, which is why I have limited myself to only school books. But now, I will start reading inspirational books in my leisure time to develop myself.

Bayo: That's my scholar. You see, personal development is very important in living a successful life. You need to understand yourself, and one thing that can help you is to carry out a SWOT analysis of yourself.

Lolu: You mean strengths, weaknesses, opportunities, and threats?

Bayo: Yes! When you carry it out, you will be able to discover your strengths to take advantage of them, your weaknesses to be able to work on them, opportunities around you to maximize them, and threats to know how to overcome them.

Lolu: I now understand personal development and why I need it for my future.

Bayo: You can develop yourself by reading inspirational books, getting someone to mentor you, watching films that will motivate you, and reading biographies and autobiographies of successful people. Remember, it takes training to reign in life.

Lolu: Thanks, my friend, for this eye-opener

Bayo: You are welcome.

CHAPTER 66

Skill Acquisition/ Vocational Studies

Bolu: Bimpe, where do you always go to every weekend that each time we call your house, we always meet your absence?

Bimpe: (*Smiles*) I always go for one vocational training programme organized by one NGO for kids and youths in the community.

Bolu: Ehn Ehn! So, what particular skill are you acquiring?

Bimpe: I am learning how to sew and string beads.

Bolu: Do you want to become a fashion designer? Is the vocation class in the school not enough for you? How do you now manage to do your assignments and house chores?

Bimpe: Well, it does not affect my studies because I get to wake up early in the morning to read and late at night. Well, as for if what they teach us in school is not enough, what they teach us in the school is just the peripheral, but I get to learn and practice more here. And to answer your question, if I want to become a fashion designer, well, I would love to, even though I will be practising my course of study at the university.

Bolu: Don't you think it is a waste of time dedicating your time and energy to it? God forbid I will become a hairdresser or a tailor after spending years in the university.

Bimpe: (*Smiles*) You see, I will not blame you because you have yet to face reality. I was thinking like you until when my brother couldn't find a job after three years of graduating. He later had to enrol in graphic designing and printing training.

Bolu: Hmm...

Bimpe: Why do you think NYSC now trains corps members in different vocational skills? Why do you think vocational studies have been introduced in schools? It is no longer news that jobs are scarce in the country now; many graduates are unemployed, and those employed are underemployed. Besides, is it not better to acquire a skill now than to wait till after graduation?

Bolu: Are you so pessimistic that you think you can't get a job in a bank or oil company after graduation?

Bimpe: You see, it is not about being pessimistic. What will I lose if I acquire the skill now and still get a job at an oil company? Besides, I can still use the skill while at home for my dresses and beads.

Bolu: Wow! I think you actually have a point; no tailor can use you to do *yanga*, oh!

Bimpe: Now you are talking.

Bolu: I hope it is not too late to join the training programme. I would like to learn how to make bags and shoes.

Bimpe: There are three months left. You can follow me this weekend, and I believe after this batch, another batch will still come up.

Bolu: Miss Bimpe, my international fashion designer.

Bimpe: That's me

Bolu: It is for me to start bringing my dresses now for you to sew.

Bimpe: Hope with money *sha*.

Bolu: But you are yet to finish the training.

Bimpe: Yes, in the next few months, I will become an international fashion designer.

CHAPTER 67

Communication skills

Titi: Ronke, why do you like beating your brother?

Ronke: The boy is so stubborn that he won't listen to simple instructions.

Titi: Beating is not the only corrective measure if someone has done something wrong; there are other better ways of correcting the person.

Ronke: Well, to me, I don't know of any better way.

Titi: You can deny him access to some programmes he likes on TV, you can report him to your dad, you can stop him from playing with his toys, you can also sit him down and talk sense to him...

Ronke: I hear you; why will I waste my saliva to be correcting someone? Didn't he know before doing it?

Titi: But instruction comes before correction. The last time Mr. Oyibo beat you, didn't you feel bad? Were you not the one complaining that he didn't even tell you your offence before flogging you? Were you, not the one who said you prefer Mr Ajayi's way of correcting students more than Mr Oyibo's because he first calls them to tell them their offence before punishing them?

Ronke: Well, I don't have time for that. You know I am a lady who only speaks a few words.

Titi: Last time I checked, you said you wanted your business to grow like that of Dangote, and now you are saying you are a lady of few words...

Ronke: What is the correlation between being a person of few words and growing my business?

Titi: Well, whatever profession you choose to pursue in life, you must be able to communicate well. Communication skills are more important in business because people will surely make you talk. You have to communicate about your product and services. It is through communication that you can convince people to buy into what you have to sell. You must be a good communicator to be in business.

Ronke: Hmm... Maybe I will have to switch my passion if that's the case.

Titi: (*Laughs*) You know the profession that I think will fit you?

Ronke: What?

Titi: You will be a good soldier. It's better you go to NDA. You are a disciplinarian and always frown.

Ronke: God forbid a bad thing; doing business is a better option. But seriously, I love being a businesswoman.

Titi: Yes, it is just for you to build your interpersonal and communication skills. You see, to be a good communicator doesn't mean you should be loquacious, and it doesn't mean you must be an orator or public speaker. It only means you can articulate the importance, benefits, and reasons why your products are good for likely consumers in a few words. Your pitch should be clear, concise, brief, and straight to the point. You can share testimonies or positive comments of customers or users about your product. You should be able to sell your products in a few minutes.

Ronke: But how do I do that?

Titi: First, you need to be a good listener to be a good communicator, you need to understand your product well, and you need to work on your temperament. When someone offends you, you take a walk to calm yourself down, like in your brother's case. Learn to always communicate your grievances or displeasure to people in a gentle manner, and understand that no one is perfect and everybody is prone to make mistakes. Learn to correct with words first rather than with a stick; feel free to say what is on your mind, and try to correct it in love.

Lastly, you can always utilize the telephone, email, business card, blogs, social media, etc. to communicate with your customers.

Ronke: Thanks, my friend, for not giving up on me.

Titi: You are welcome, friend.

CHAPTER 68

Entrepreneurship and Economy Growth

Teacher: Good morning, students.

Class: Good morning, Mr Thomas.

Teacher: I believe you are all doing great, as I can see your shining faces. I would like to sample your opinion; what can you say about this country?

Venita: Sir, I am tired of this country; I have not eaten this morning, and my parents have not been paid a salary for the past three months.

Nuhu: Your own is even better; my dad was laid off five months ago, and we have only been living on the meagre salary my mum is earning.

Chioma: But sir, why are things not working here? Many youths are trying to get a visa to go abroad to any country. Many youths die in the desert trying to escape to other countries for greener pastures.

Abashi: Just some months back, some Nigerians were killed due to xenophobic attacks by some South Africans; if the country were to be okay, I doubt if Nigerians would have reasons to travel out. They would rather be the ones coming here.

Clarimond: This country seems not to be working; I was told by my parents that the Naira used to be stronger than the dollar, but now $1 is equivalent to ₦1400 or more, while even Ghana's Cedi is stronger than our Naira. But why is this so, sir?

James: I once had a discussion with my dad on value addition; he told me that even though Nigeria is blessed with many natural and mineral resources, we are still poor compared to other developed nations. We sell these resources to them in their crude form, and they sell back to us at higher prices after they have added value to them. I believe that is why they have a better economy, and people want to go there.

Teacher: I am so happy with all the salient points you have all made; this is why I will quickly be talking about entrepreneurship and the economy. You see, no country develops as a consuming economy but as a producing economy. One major difference between Nigeria and other developed nations of the world is that those nations are producing nations while we are only consuming. These nations produce, innovate, manufacture goods, and take the risk of venturing into new terrains. They spend on research and development, they promote creativity and encourage ingenuity, but we are after buying from them for our consumption. They breed entrepreneurs while we breed consumers.

Nuhu: So, entrepreneurs can identify opportunities, explore, and take the risk of harnessing their resources to produce goods and services.

Teacher: Exactly! Entrepreneurs can control and coordinate all other production factors, such as land, labour, and capital, to produce goods and services. Entrepreneurs can identify what to produce that people will need, why to produce them, how to produce them, who to produce them for, and where to produce them. These are the basic questions that an entrepreneur tries to solve.

Venita: How do I become an entrepreneur?

Teacher: You see, to become an entrepreneur, you must be able to discover yourself, your strengths, talents, potential, and passion. You should be able to develop yourself, and all you have to do is add value to the people and society. You should be able to package what you have to appeal to people and take the risk of commercializing or exchanging it for money.

Chioma: How can entrepreneurs affect the economy of a nation?

Teacher: That is a beautiful question. I will relate it to what James said earlier. The more people are ready to create new things or repackage existing things in a better way to add more value, the more the society will develop, and more jobs will be created. The country becomes self-sufficient and relies less on imported goods. When the country exports and makes more money, more tourists will be attracted. Through this, the government will generate more taxes; the more the government can do for the citizens, the more life becomes pleasurable and enjoyable to the citizens, leading to an increase in their life span. There are so many benefits a country enjoys when there are entrepreneurs in a country.

James: But if this is so, sir, why don't we have many entrepreneurs in this country?

Teacher: Many factors are responsible. Many people have not been thoroughly taught how to become an entrepreneur, which is why we are treating it now. Many people still believe entrepreneurship is for low-class people and illiterates. Besides, people believe that going to school and having a certificate guarantees success in life. Others who ventured into it did so out of desperation, either because they couldn't get a white-collar job or because they saw others thriving in it without carrying out a background check and self-evaluation, which made them fail. Some are scared of taking the risk. Many factors are actually responsible.

Clarimond: So, in essence, other developed countries have been able to give room for entrepreneurship to thrive by creating the right environment.

Teacher: Exactly! If you look at the record, you will see that the USA's economy is largely built on small-scale and medium-scale entrepreneurs. For the economy of Nigeria to grow and for life to become better for all, we need more entrepreneurs who will not wait for a white-collar job or pay jobs. In conclusion, we need more entrepreneurs in this country who will dare to take the risk of starting something innovative and creative that will add value to people and develop this nation, look beyond the problems and limitations around but see possibilities and opportunities,

CHAPTER 69

Bounce Back from Business Setback

Andy: Good morning, my Taiwo; why is my beautiful wife not looking cheerful?

Taiwo: She has been complaining about her business, not doing well to me.

Kenny: Yes, I am tired of this business. The sales had really dropped. Customers are no longer showing up. Those who show up haggle the price anyhow, those who even want to buy at the actual price want to buy on credit, and those who buy on credit fail to pay at the time due unless you start chasing them up and down. You can see how my shop is empty of goods and capital stuck in the hands of debtors. I'm just not cut out for business.

Taiwo: Hmm... I can relate to what you are talking about; eyes have seen a lot in business. You deal with people of different shades and attitudes; some don't care if your business collapses as long as their own needs are met. Some will price your goods below the goods' cost price; some will buy things beyond their credit limit and start avoiding you when they know the time to pay has matured. When they need the items, they would be crying up and down, displaying the 'pretentious' innocent look and saying all manners of things that you would be forced to have mercy on them and sell on credit to them, but when you check on them for the money, they make you look like a wicked person. It's one of the challenges one faces in business.

Kenny: Seriously, it is very annoying and frustrating.

Taiwo: Yes, I told you I have been there before. Things went so bad that some friends advised me to quit the business.

Kenny: Really, that's true, I remember, but how did you overcome it?

Taiwo: Well, the first thing I did was go back to Uncle John, who registered me for a business seminar so I could acquire more training and business skills. I heard lots of practical tips and stories that changed my mindset on how to do business. Secondly, I consulted with my friend Andy. From the information I gathered, my business has been able to experience a paradigm shift.

Kenny: Hmm... Thank God you are both here now; I am pretty sure you guys will share some of those tips with me.

Andy: Well, you will first have to pay a consultancy fee. You know nothing valuable is free, not even in Freetown.

Taiwo: Ah Ahn! What are friends for? Is it every time you collect money, remember she is your wife, and I'm your brother-in-law?

Andy: (*Smiles*) Just kidding, how would I charge money from my wife-to-be?

Kenny: (*Smiles*) Leave me. This is a business transaction, and you want to drag family into it. Let me get my writing materials to jot down sensible things.

Andy: Okay, sweetheart, you see, you may not understand the effects of some of these things, but they work most of the time for people. The first thing is to stay positive, no matter the challenges. You cannot win if you have not won within. Thomas Edison tried several times to invent the bulb but kept failing; when asked if he was a failure, he said he didn't fail but only learnt another way of not doing it. The second tip is to have a clear mental picture of what, where, and how you desire your business to be. Growth and development start from within. You see, there is what is called the law of attraction; what you have in your mind has a way of gravitating towards you. The third tip is to always speak positively about your business, always declare what you desire, and don't speak negatively about your business. Even when customers are not coming, don't complain; declare what you want to see. The power of life and death is in the tongue; you can kill your business with your mouth and grow it with your mouth. You see, this is the beginning of greatness. After you have settled it within you, other things can follow.

Kenny: To be honest, I have defaulted in these three areas, but with this, I hope to adjust and have a mental shift. Are there any other tips?

Andy: The place of good customer service cannot be swept under the carpet. Be innovative and creative in how you arrange your goods, use a different approach in advertising on social media, be value-conscious, not just money-conscious, maintain proper books of account, be happy and passionate with what you do, be careful of credit sales, sell at a reasonable profit rate so your goods will not be too expensive and most importantly, commit your business into God's hand.

Kenny: Seriously, you have made my day. I have really learnt a lot from you this morning,

Taiwo: I will help you bring the videos and materials I got from the business seminar to learn more.

Kenny: Thanks, bro! What can I use to entertain you guys now? Let me quickly get you something.

Andy: Before you go, remember quitters don't win, and winners don't quit. Tough times never last, but tough people do. That's why I will never give up on you, my beautiful wife.

Kenny: (*Smiles*) Are you sure you can afford me? My bride price includes aeroplane...

(*All laugh*)

CHAPTER 70

The G-Factor

Ibrahim: Usman, it's time for Jum'at prayers, let's go.

Usman: I am not going today, as I am leaving school now; I must get to the orchard before the owner leaves for the mosque so that I can supply my customers before 4 o'clock. This should give me enough time to study for the exams that start on Monday.

Titi: Businessman, we Yorubas have a saying, *'What is good needs prayers and the one that is yet to be good needs prayers too.'* There is nothing we can achieve without the help of God.

Usman: I know we need God's help, but will He come down to do what we have to do for us? No man can succeed without hard work and check the developed nations of the world; they are not as religious as we are, yet they have a thriving economy; in fact, many inventors and entrepreneurs don't go to church or mosque. Every second I have is golden.

Titi: I am not disputing the fact that we must do our part by working hard, but only God can guarantee the success of a thing. Paul can plant, and Apollos can water, but only God can give the increase. There is a proverb that says, *'For man to labour and enjoy the rewards of his labour, it is a gift from the Lord.'* It is one thing for a man to work hard, and it is another for him to be able to enjoy the fruits of his labour. There is a farmer who worked hard and had a great harvest from his farm, but because he neglected the owner of his soul, he couldn't enjoy what he laboured for.

Usman: Is God not wicked to have taken away the farmer's life after he had worked hard with results to show?

Titi: On the contrary, God is good and merciful. He wants us to have all the good things of life to enjoy; He only hates pride, which is why He wants us to always stay humble and acknowledge Him in all we do. So, it is not about being religious, but always appreciating God for the gift of life He has given us and the privilege even to work and have results to show.

Ibrahim: Tell him, he knows what the Holy Quran says: *'And Allah has made for you from that which He had created, shadows, and has made from you from the mountains, shelter, and has made for you garments which protect you from heat and garments which protects you from your [enemy in] battle. Thus, does He complete His favour upon you that you might submit [to Him].' 'O mankind, remember the favour of Allah upon you. Is there any creator other than Allah who provides for you from the heavens and earth? There is no deity except Him, so how are you deluded?'*

Titi: Ah, Usman! So, you know what the Holy Quran says, and you are still placing other things before God? It is only God that makes everything possible. You can't have anything in life unless God ordains it, and neither can your hard work amount to anything except He allows it. There is the story of a Nigerian entrepreneur that I heard; he went to Benin at a point when a prophet of God came to request two persons to please stand up for his guest. This young businessman stood up with his PA, and the prophet blessed him with the promise that he would become a household name and his business would spread across Africa. Today, it has become so. Every house in Nigeria uses his products.

Usman: Are you kidding me? Could that not be a mere coincidence?

Ibrahim: There is nothing God cannot do. Undoubtedly, we need to read, study, learn, and work hard, but we must put God first, just like the Americans will always say, "In God we trust," and their economy is doing well.

Usman: Okay, let's go together; after all, we won't spend more than thirty minutes.

Ibrahim: Don't worry. We will divide the labour to attend to all our customers simultaneously.

Titi: Include me in your prayers.

The end!

ACTION PLAN

Get a book/jotter you can write down the following.

1. Mention ten key things you have learnt from this book.

2. What are your innate abilities, talents, potentials, natural gifting you have discovered about yourself? Things you have flair for or do with ease.

3. Mention some of the problems and challenges you see around you: family, society and nation as a whole.

4. Match your talent, potential and natural ability with one or two of the problems you have listed.

5. Write down your vision, dreams and aspiration.

6. Is there any connection between your goals, vision and aspiration and your talents, natural abilities and potentials?

7. Have you discovered any successful individual along the path of your dream and aspirations?

8. Have you read about their biography, autobiographies, books, writings and other secrets you can find about them if you don't have direct links to them? If not, be deliberate and intention in doing so.

9. Mention some of the skills/training/self-development programmes you need that can help you develop or sharpen your talents and potentials.

10. What are the unnecessary things you spend money on or time-wasting activities that you indulge in and need to cut down and what investments move are you making towards your desired future?

Don't think money first, don't think fame first and don't think comfort first, rather, think about solution to problems, think about how you can add value to people and things around you, think first about how you can make imparts in your family and the society at large then money, fame and comfort will come running.